THE BRONTË FAMILY

WITH SPECIAL REFERENCE TO
PATRICK BRANWELL BRONTË

VOL. I.

BY

FRANCIS A. LEYLAND

IN TWO VOLUMES.

VOL. I.

First published in 1886

British Library Cataloguing-in-Publication Data
A catalogue record for this book is available
from the British Library

CONTENTS

PREFACE.

It has long seemed to me that the history of the Brontë family is incomplete, and, in some senses, not well understood. Those who have written upon it—as I shall have occasion to point out in these pages—have had certain objects in view, which have, perhaps necessarily, led them to give undue weight to special points and to overlook others. Thus it happens that, though there are in the hands of the public several able works on the Brontës, there are many circumstances relating to them that are yet in comparative obscurity. Especially has injustice been done to one member of the family—Patrick Branwell Brontë—whose life has several times been treated by those who have had some other object in view; and, through a misunderstanding of the character of the brother, the sisters, Anne in particular, have been put, in some respects, in a false light also. This circumstance, coupled with the fact that I am in possession of much new information, and am able to print here a considerable quantity of unknown poetry from Branwell's hand, has induced me to write this work. Those of his poems which are included in these volumes are placed in dealing with the periods of his life in which they were written, for I felt that, however great might be the advantages of putting them together in a complete form, much more would be lost both to the interest of the poems and the life of their author in doing so. Branwell's poems, more, perhaps, than those of any other writer, are so clearly expressive of his feelings at the time of their writing, that a correct view of his character is only to be obtained by looking upon them as parts of his life-history, which indeed they are. And, moreover, when we consider the circumstances under which any of these were written, our understanding and appreciation of the subject must necessarily be much fuller and truer. It has not escaped the attention of writers on the Brontë story that Branwell had an important influence on his sisters; and, though I maintain it to have been essentially different from what others allege, it would not be possible to do justice either to him or to them without saying a good deal about his character.

I have felt it right, in these pages, to some extent also, to reconsider the character of the Rev. Patrick Brontë, which has, along with that of his son, suffered unfair treatment in the biographies of his daughters. I have likewise entered upon some account of the local circumstances of art and literature which surrounded the Brontës, an element in their history which has hitherto been unknown, but is especially necessary to a right understanding of the life and work of Branwell Brontë and his sisters. These circumstances, and the altered view I have taken of the tone of the lives of Mr. Brontë and his son, have obliged me to deal more fully than would otherwise have been necessary with the early years of the Brontës, but I venture to hope that this may be atoned for by the new light I have thus been enabled to throw on some important points. There are published here, for the first time, a series of letters which Branwell Brontë addressed to an intimate friend, J. B. Leyland, sculptor, who died in 1851, and it is with these that a fresh insight is obtained into an interesting period of Branwell's life.

I am largely indebted in some parts of my work, especially those which deal with the lives of the sisters, to Mrs. Gaskell's fascinating 'Life of Charlotte Brontë'; and it is a source of sincere regret to me that I am compelled to differ from that writer on many points. I am likewise indebted in parts to Mr. T. Wemyss Reid's admirable 'Charlotte Brontë: a Monograph,' a work which has corrected several errors and misconceptions into which Mrs. Gaskell had fallen. The reader will perceive that I am obliged in several places to combat the theories and question the statements of Miss A. Mary F. Robinson in her 'Emily Brontë,' a book which, nevertheless, so far as its special subject is concerned, is a worthy contribution to the history of the Brontës.

I have also found of much use, in writing this work, an article entitled 'Branwell Brontë,' which Mr. George Searle Phillips— 'January Searle'—published in the 'Mirror' in 1872. The chapter in Mr. Francis H. Grundy's 'Pictures of the Past' on Branwell Brontë, has likewise been of the greatest service to me. Both these gentlemen were Branwell's personal friends, and to them I gladly acknowledge my indebtedness.

Among many other sources of information respecting the Brontës, of which I have availed myself in writing these pages, I may mention *Hours at Home*, 'Unpublished Letters of Charlotte Brontë'; *Scribner*, 'Reminiscences of Charlotte Brontë'; the *Athenæum*, 'Notices and Letters,' by Mr. A. C. Swinburne, and 'One of the Survivors of the Brontë-Branwell Family.' To this lady I must also express my obligation for her very kind letter to me.

In the preparation of my work I have been greatly assisted by the information, and encouraged by the sympathy, of several who had personal knowledge of Patrick Branwell Brontë, and who have supported the view I have taken of his life and character, and also who had like knowledge of the other members of the Brontë family. Among these, I have to express my sincere thanks to Mr. H. Merrall and to Mr. William Wood, who were early acquaintances of Branwell; also to Mr. William Dearden. To Mr. J. H. Thompson and Mrs. Thornton I am greatly indebted for information respecting Branwell's sojourn in Bradford. I have likewise derived much information from the family of the Browns, now all deceased, except Mrs. Brown, to whom I have to express my obligation. I have also gained much reliable information from Nancy Garrs, now Mrs. Wainwright, the nurse of the Brontës, and to her I must especially express my thanks. To these, I must not omit to add my deep and sincere thanks to those who will not permit me to mention them by name, for the unwearied assistance, counsel, and literary judgment which they have as cheerfully, as they have ably, rendered.

F. A. L.

Oakwood, Skircoat, Halifax,
October, 1885.

CHAPTER I.

EARLY CIRCUMSTANCES OF THE BRONTËS.

Brontë Genius—Brontë—Birthplace—early
Endeavours——to Hartshead—Town—Courtship and
Marriage—to Thornton—House—Chapel—. Brontë's
failing Health—. Brontë Accepts the Living of Haworth—
of the Inhabitants—Local Fights between Haworth and
Heptonstall—of Haworth—. Brontë dies.

Not many stories of literary success have attracted so much
interest, and are in themselves so curious and enthralling, as that
of the Brontë sisters. The question has often been asked how it
came about that these children, who were brought up in distant
solitude, and cut off, in a manner, from intellectual life, who had
but a partial opportunity of studying mankind, and scarcely any
knowledge of the ways of the outside world, were enabled, with
searching hands, to dissect the finest meshes of the passions,
to hold up in the clearest light the springs of human action,
and to depict, with nervous power, the most masculine and
forcible aspects of character. The solution has been sought in the
initiatory strength and inherent mental disposition of the sisters,
framed and moulded by the weird and rugged surroundings of
their youth, and tinged with lurid light and vivid feeling by the
misfortunes and sins of their unhappy brother. To illustrate
these several points, the biographers of Charlotte and Emily
Brontë have explained, as the matter admitted of explanation,
the intellectual beginnings and capability of the sisters, have
painted in sombre colours the story of their friendless childhood,

9

and lastly, with no lack of honest condemnation, have told us as much as they knew of the sad history of Patrick Branwell Brontë, their brother. It is a curious fact that this brother, who was looked upon by his family as its brightest ornament and hope, should be named in these days only in connection with his sisters, and then but with apology, condemnation, or reproach. In the course of this work, in which Branwell Brontë will be traced from his parentage to his death, we shall find the explanation of this circumstance; but we shall find, also, that, despite his failings and his sins, his intellectual gifts, as they are testified by his literary promise and his remains, entitle him to a high place as a worthy member of that extraordinary family. It will be seen, moreover, that his influence upon Charlotte, Emily, and Anne was not what has been generally supposed, and that other circumstances, besides their own domestic troubles, inspired them to write their masterpieces.

The father of these gifted authors, Patrick Brontë, whose life and personal characteristics well deserve study, was a native of the county Down. He was born on St. Patrick's Day, 1777; and, after an infancy passed at the house of his father, Hugh Brontë, or Brunty, at Ahaderg—one of the ten children who made a noisy throng in the home of his parents—he opened, at the age of sixteen, a village school at Drumgooland, in the same county. In this occupation he continued after he had attained his majority, and was never a tutor, as Mrs. Gaskell supposes; but, being ambitious of a clerical life, through the assistance of his patron, Mr. Tighe, incumbent of Drumgooland and Drumballyroony, in the county of Down, he was admitted to St. John's College, Cambridge, on the 1st of October in the year 1802, when he had attained his twenty-fifth year. At Cambridge we may infer that he led an active life. It is known that he joined a volunteer corps raised to be in readiness for the French invasion, threatened at the time. After a four years' sojourn at his college, having graduated as a bachelor of arts, in the year 1806, he was ordained, and appointed to a curacy in Essex, where he is said not to have stayed long.

The perpetual curacy of Hartshead, in the West-Riding of Yorkshire, having become vacant, Mr. Brontë received the appointment, on the presentation of the vicar of Dewsbury. The church of St. Peter, at Hartshead—which has extensive remains of Norman work, and has recently been restored—is situated on an eminence about a mile from the actual hamlet of that name; and, with its broad, low, and massive tower, and its grim old yew-tree, forms a conspicuous object for miles around, commanding on all sides extensive and magnificent views of the valleys of Calder and Colne, with their wooded slopes, and pleasant farms, and the busy villages nestling in the hollows. At the foot of the hill, the deep and sombre woods of Kirklees hide the almost indistinguishable remains of the convent, founded by Raynerus Flandrensis, in the reign of Henry II., for nuns of the order of Citeaux.

There are interesting circumstances and evidences concerning Kirklees, its Roman entrenchments being very distinct within the park which overlooks the Calder at this point. The priory, too, has its curious history of the events which attended the cloistered life of Elizabeth de Stainton, one of the prioresses, whose monumental memorial alone remains of all that marked the graves of the religious of that house; and there are stories relating to Robin Hood. Here still exists the chamber in which tradition says the 'noble outlaw' died, and also the grave, at a cross-bow shot from it, where long generations of men have averred his dust reposes. The district of Kirklees had an interest for Charlotte Brontë, and she has celebrated it in 'Shirley,' under the name of Nunnely, with its old church, its forest, its monastic ruins, and 'its man of title—its baronet.' It was to the house of the latter—kind gentleman though he was—that Louis Moore could not go, where he 'would much sooner have made an appointment with the ghost of the Earl of Huntingdon to meet him, and a shadowy ring of his merry men, under the canopy of the thickest, blackest, oldest oak in Nunnely Forest ... would rather have appointed tryst with a phantom abbess, or mist-pale nun, among the wet and weedy relics of that ruined sanctuary of theirs, mouldering in the core of the wood.'

Mr. Brontë entered upon his ministrations at Hartshead in the year 1811; and there are entries in the churchwarden's book of Easter-dues paid to him up to 1815. It is curious to note that, in this early mention of Mr. Brontë, the name is spelled 'Brunty' and 'Bronty.'

Hartshead being destitute of a glebe house, and no suitable residence existing either at this place or at the neighbouring village of Clifton at the time, Mr. Brontë took up his residence at High Town, in a roomy and pleasant house at the top of Clough Lane, near Liversedge in the parish of Birstall, and about a mile from the place of his cure. The house, which commands beautiful views, is entered by a passage of the ordinary width, on the left of which is the drawing-room, having cross-beams ornamented with plaster mouldings, as when first finished. On the right of the passage is the dining-room. The breakfast-room and kitchen are behind them. The house is three stories in height, and stands back about two yards from the road, which points direct to the now populous towns of Liversedge and Cleckheaton, both places of considerable antiquity, whose inhabitants, employed in various manufacturies, were increasing in Mr. Brontë's time.

Finding himself now in possession of a competent income and a goodly residence, he felt relieved from those anxieties which, in all probability, had attended his early struggles; and, resting awhile in his ambition, he turned in peace and contentment to poetical meditation. His first book was called 'Cottage Poems,' on the title-page of which he describes himself as the 'Reverend Patrick Brontë, B.A., minister of Hartshead-cum-Clifton.' This book was published at Halifax in the year 1811. The following are a few of its subjects: 'The Happy Cottagers,' 'The Rainbow,' 'Winter Nights' Meditations,' 'Verses sent to a Lady on her Birthday,' 'The Cottage Maid,' and 'The Spider and the Fly.' Mr. Brontë thus speaks of himself and his work: 'When relieved from clerical avocations he was occupied in writing the "Cottage Poems;" from morning till noon, and from noon till night, his employment was full of indescribable pleasure, such as he could wish to taste as long as life lasts. His hours glided pleasantly and almost imperceptibly by, and when night drew on, and he retired to rest, ere his eyes closed in sleep with sweet calmness and serenity of mind, he often reflected that, though the delicate palate of criticism might be disgusted, the business of the day in the prosecution of his humble task was well-pleasing in the sight of God, and by His blessing might be rendered useful to some poor soul who cared little about critical niceties.' Throughout he professes to be indifferent to hostile criticism.

It is pleasant to find that Mr. Brontë, although settled in competence in a picturesque part of England, was not forgetful of his parents or of the land of his birth. So long as his mother lived he sent her twenty pounds a year; and, though we have no record of the occasion, we may safely infer that he found opportunity to visit Ireland again. He maintained his connection with the district of his early life; and, in after-years, he appointed a relative of Mr. Tighe to be his own curate. One of his 'Cottage Poems' is entitled 'The Irish Cabin,' a verse or two from which may here be given:—

'Should poverty, modest and clean,
E'er please when presented to view,
Should cabin on brown heath or green,
Disclose aught engaging to you;
Should Erin's wild harp soothe the ear,
When touched by such fingers as mine,
Then kindly attentive draw near,
And candidly ponder each line.'

He describes a winter-scene on the mountains of Morne—a high range of hills in the north of Ireland—and thus alludes to his hospitable reception in the clean and industrious cabin of his verses:—

> 'Escaped from the pitiless storm,
> I entered the humble retreat;
> Compact was the building, and warm,
> In furniture simple and neat.
> And now, gentle reader, approve
> The ardour that glowed in each breast,
> As kindly our cottagers strove
> To cherish and welcome their guest.'

It is unnecessary to give in this place further extracts from this book; suffice it to say that, in all probability, Mr. Brontë lived to see the day when he was pained and surprised that he had ever committed it to the press.

Although the poems of Mr. Brontë are inspired by the love of a peaceful and contented life, free from excitement and care, yet in times of trouble and emergency, such as those of the Luddite riots which occurred during the period of his ministration at Hartshead, he showed again the active and resolute spirit which had prompted and sustained the efforts of his early ambition; and his ardour in helping to suppress the turbulent spirit of the neighbourhood would have made him very unpopular with the disaffected people, had they not learned to respect the upright and unfailing rectitude of his conduct. In the energetic character of Mr. Brontë's life in these early times, in his persistent ambition, and in the literary pursuits which clearly were dear to him, we may trace those factors of working power and literary aspiration and taste which made up the characteristic intellectual force of his children.

Mrs. Gaskell, in her 'Life of Charlotte Brontë,' has given some of the particulars of the Reverend Mr. Brontë's courtship and marriage, in which she appears to have taken a lively interest.

Mr. Brontë met his future wife, (Miss Maria Branwell—of whose character I shall speak in the next chapter—the third daughter of Mr. T. Branwell of Penzance, deceased) for the first time about the summer of 1812, when she was on a visit to her uncle, the Rev. John Fennel, a Methodist minister and head-master of the Wesleyan Academy at Woodhouse Grove, near Bradford, but who became later a clergyman of the Establishment, and was made incumbent of Cross-stone, in the parish of Halifax. This meeting was soon followed by an engagement, and, says Mrs. Gaskell, there were plans for happy picnic-parties to Kirkstall Abbey in the glowing September days, when 'Uncle, Aunt, and Cousin Jane'—the last engaged to a Mr. Morgan, another clergyman—were of the party.

In the account which Mr. Brontë gives of the aim and scope of the work from which I have made an extract, and the state of his mind while engaged upon it, we have a retrospect of the inner life of the father of the Brontës, during his sojourn at Hartshead as perpetual curate, prior to his marriage with Miss Branwell. In this period of his life, he seems to have been perfectly happy, no cloud or anticipation of future sorrow having obscured or diminished the fulness of his peace. The marriage was celebrated on the 29th of December, 1812, at Guiseley, near Bradford, by the Rev. W. Morgan, minister of Bierley, the gentleman engaged to 'Cousin Jane.' It is a very curious circumstance that on the same day, and at the same place, Mr. Brontë performed the marriage ceremony between his wife's cousin, Miss Jane Fennel, only daughter of the Mr. Fennel alluded to above, and the Rev. W. Morgan, who had just been, as described, the officiating clergyman at his own wedding.

Mr. Fennel would naturally have performed the ceremony for his niece and Mr. Brontë, had it not fallen to his lot to give the lady away.

When Mr. Brontë found himself settled in married life at Hartshead, and with the probability of a young family rising around him, he felt pleasure in the contemplation of the future. Mrs. Brontë, ever gentle and affectionate in her household ways, comforted and encouraged him in his literary pursuits, and, by her acute observation and accurate judgment, directed and aided his own. It was at this time that Mr. Brontë wrote a book, entitled 'The Rural Ministry,' which was published at Halifax, in 1813. The work consisted of a miscellany of descriptive poems, with the following titles: 'The Sabbath Bells,' 'Kirkstall Abbey,' 'Extempore Verses,' 'Lines to a Lady on her Birthday,' 'An Elegy,' 'Reflections by Moonlight,' 'Winter,' 'Rural Happiness,' 'The Distress and Relief,' 'The Christian's Farewell,' 'The Harper of Erin.' It cannot be doubted that, in consequence of his two publications while he was at Hartshead, Mr. Brontë became known in the surrounding districts as an aspiring man, and one of literary culture and ability.

Mr. Brontë had taken his bride to his house at High Town, and it was there that his daughters Maria and Elizabeth were born. Maria was baptized on April the 23rd, 1814, and is entered in the register as the 'daughter of Patrick Brontë and Maria his wife.' The Rev. Mr. Morgan was the officiating minister. There is no such entry there relating to Elizabeth, for she was baptized at Thornton with the other children.

Mr. Brontë, after having been nearly five years minister of Hartshead-cum-Clifton, resigned the benefice, and accepted, from the vicar of Bradford, the incumbency of Thornton, a perpetual curacy in that parish. This, probably, on the suggestion of Mr. Morgan, who was then incumbent of Christ's Church at Bradford.

Thornton is beautifully situated on the northern slope of a valley. Green and fertile pastures spread over the adjacent hills, and wooded dells with shady walks beautify and enrich the district. 'The neighbourhood,' says Mrs. Gaskell, 'is desolate and wild; great tracts of bleak land, enclosed by stone dykes, sweeping up Clayton Heights.' This disagreeable picture of the place, painted by the biographer of Charlotte, is scarcely justified by the actual appearance of the district. The soil is naturally fertile, and the inhabitants are notable for industry and enterprise. Hence no barren land, within the wide range of hill and vale, is now seen obtruding on the cultivated sweep.

The town is somewhat regularly built. In the main street is situated the house where Mr. Brontë took up his abode during his stay at Thornton. The hall door was reached by several steps. There was a dining-room on one side of the hall, and a drawing-room on the other. Over the passage to the front was a dressing-room, at the window of which the neighbours often saw Mr. Brontë at his toilet. Above the door of the house, on a stone slab, there are still visible the letters:

A.

J.   S.

1802

These are the initials of John and Sarah Ashworth, former inhabitants of Thornton; and this residence remained as the parsonage until another was built below, nearer to the chapel, by the successor of Mr. Brontë.

The chapel of Thornton is a narrow, contracted, and unsightly building. The north side is lighted by two rows of square cottage windows—on the south side, five late perpendicular pointed windows permit the sun to relieve the gloom of the interior.

The diminutive communion-table is lighted by a four-mullioned window, above which, externally, in the wall, appears the date 1620. The interior is blocked, on the ground floor, with high-backed, unpainted deal pews. Two galleries hide the windows almost from view, and cast a gloom over the interior of the edifice. The area under the pews, and in the aisles, is paved with gravestones, and a fetid, musty smell floats through the damp and mouldering interior. In this chapel, Mr. Brontë preached and ministered, and from the pulpit, placed high above the curate and clerk, whence he delivered his sermons, he could see his wife and children in a pew just below him.

The new incumbent of Thornton seems to have taken active

interest in his chapel; for in the western screen, which divides a kind of lobby from the nave, is painted, on a wooden tablet, an inscription recording that in the year 1818 this chapel was 'Repaired and Beautified,' the Rev. Patrick Brontë, B.A., being then minister.

While at Thornton Mr. Brontë steadily pursued his literary avocations, one of his books being a small volume entitled, 'The Cottage in the Wood, or the Art of becoming Rich and Happy.' This is an account of a pious family, consisting of an aged couple and a virtuous child, whose appearance and education qualify her for a higher position in the world than that of a cottager's daughter. Accident brings to their door a young man in a state of almost helpless drunkenness, whose habits are the most profligate and dissolute, as the sequel discloses; and the object of the book is to show the dire consequences of continued intemperance. The story is told in prose, but Mr. Brontë gives a poetical version of one event in the narrative. It is entitled, 'The Nightly Revel,' and possesses a dignity of its own. The following extract shows considerable improvement, in diction and verse, upon the style of his small volume published at Halifax, in 1811. For this reason it is well worth reproducing.

'Around the table polish'd goblets shine,
Fill'd with brown ale, or crown'd with ruddy wine;
Each quaffs his glass, and, thirsty, calls for more,
Till maddening mirth, and song, and wild uproar,
And idly fierce dispute, and brutal fight
Break the soft slumbers of the peaceful night.

'Without, within, above, beneath, around,
Ungodly jests and deep-mouthed oaths resound;
Pale Reason, trembling, leaves her reeling throne,
Truth, Honour, Virtue, Justice, all are flown;
The sly, dark-glancing harlot's fatal breath
Allures to sin and sorrow, shame and death.

The gaming-table, too, that fatal snare,
Beset with fiercest passions fell is there;
Remorse, despair, revenge, and deadly hate,
With dark design, in bitter durance wait,
Till Scarlet Murder waves his bloody hand,
Gives in sepulchral tone the dread command;
Then forth they rush, and from the secret sheath
Draw the keen blade and do the work of death.'

Mr. Brontë also, in 1818, before his appointment to Haworth, published his 'Maid of Killarney.' He had not been long at Thornton, where he went about the year 1815, when a considerable increase in his family added to his parental responsibilities.

On his acceptance of the living, he probably enjoyed a larger stipend than at Hartshead, but the demands of a young family, perhaps, on the whole, made him a poorer man. There Charlotte Brontë was born in April, 1816; Patrick Branwell Brontë in 1817; Emily Jane Brontë in 1818; and Anne Brontë probably just before Mr. Brontë's removal to Haworth, which was on February 25th, 1820, as we are told by Mrs. Gaskell.

Of the life of the Brontës at Thornton we know little. But there were causes of anxiety pressing on Mr. Brontë at the time. The state of his wife's health was a real sorrow, and although he derived solace from his literary pursuits and the society of his clerical friends, his spirits were damped by the contemplation of the season of bereavement and affliction that assuredly threatened him at no distant date.

With six young children, who might soon become motherless, Mr. Brontë's future was dark and discouraging, and he entertained the idea of resigning, at no distant day, the then place of his cure. Here, living within a reasonable distance of Bradford, he had an opportunity of moving in a larger circle of friends than at Hartshead, and it was here that his children received their earliest impressions of local life and character. Old inhabitants of Thornton remembered them playing in the space opposite their father's residence, in the village street, and had often seen them carried, or their parents lead them by the hand, in the lanes of the neighbourhood. They were children only when they left Thornton; yet, on many grounds, the inhabitants of that village may feel privileged that it was the birthplace of the authors of 'Jane Eyre,' 'Wuthering Heights,' and 'The Tenant of Wildfell Hall.'

Shortly an opportunity presented itself to Mr. Brontë for leaving Thornton, a vacancy having taken place at Haworth through the death of the curate, Mr. Charnock. The situation of this chapelry was blessed with a more bracing air, and the curate had a somewhat better stipend than Thornton allowed, and so Mr. Brontë accepted the presentation from the patron. We are informed, however, that, on visiting the place of his intended ministrations, he was told that while to him personally the parishioners had no objection, yet, as the nominee of the vicar of Bradford, he would not be received. He had no idea that the inhabitants had a veto in the appointment.

On Mr. Brontë declaring that, if he had not the good-will of the inhabitants, his ministrations would be useless, the place was presented to Mr. Redhead by the patron, and the village seems to have become the scene of extraordinary proceedings. It appears that, after the Reformation, the presentation to the curacy of Haworth, which had been from time immemorial vested in the vicar of Bradford, had become subject to the control of the freeholders, and of certain trustees who held possession of the principal funds from which the stipend of the curate proceeded, which they could withhold, by virtue of an authority they appear to have been empowered with. In effect, they could at any time disallow or render void an appointment, if disagreeable to themselves, by keeping back the stipend. Mr. Brontë, writing later of Mr. Redhead, says of this: 'My predecessor took the living with the consent of the vicar of Bradford and certain trustees, in consequence of which he was so opposed that, after only three weeks' possession, he was compelled to resign.' What this opposition and its immediate effects were, we learn from the pages of Mrs. Gaskell's 'Life of Charlotte Brontë,' and they may be mentioned here as illustrative of the pre-eminent resolution and force of character which ever distinguish the inhabitants of the West-Riding and the dwellers on these rough-hewn and storm-beaten elevations.

During the long illness which preceded the death of Mr. Charnock, incumbent of Haworth, his assistant curate, Mr. Redhead, had supplied his place; who, on Mr. Brontë's withdrawal, was presented, as is stated above, to the vacant living by the patron, and he seems to have been determined to hold the chapelry, *vi et armis*, in defiance of the inhabitants. But the freeholders, conceiving they had been deprived of their long established prerogative, or an attempt was being made to interfere with it, protested against Mr. Redhead's appointment. On the first occasion of this gentleman's preaching in the church, it was crowded not by worshippers, but by a multitude of people bent on mischief. These resolved the service should not proceed, or that it should be rendered inaudible. To secure this object they had put on the heavy wooden clogs they daily wore, except on Sundays, and, while the surpliced minister was reading the opening service, the stamping and clattering of the clogs drowned his voice, and the people left the church, making all the noise and uproar that was in their power, which was by no means feeble. The following Sunday witnessed proceedings still more disgraceful. We are told that at the commencement of the service, a man rode up the nave of the church on an ass, with his face to the tail, and with a number of old hats piled on his head. On urging his beast forward, the screams of delight, the roars of laughter, and the shouts of the approving conspirators completely drowned the clergyman's voice; and he left the chapel, but not yet discomfited.

Mr. Redhead, on the third Sunday, resolved to make a strenuous and final effort to keep the ecclesiastical citadel of which he had been formally put in possession. For this purpose he brought with him a body of cavalry, composed of a number of sympathising gentlemen, with their horses; and the curate, thus accompanied by his supporters, ascended the village street and put up at the 'Bull.' But the enemy had been on the alert: the people were exasperated, and followed the new-comers to the church, accompanied by a chimney-sweep who had, not long before, finished his labours at some adjacent chimneys, and whom they had made half drunk. Him they placed right before the reading-desk, which Mr. Redhead had already reached, and the drunken, black-faced sweep nodded assent to the measured utterances of the minister. 'At last,' it is said, 'either prompted by some mischief-maker, or from some tipsy impulse, he clambered up the pulpit stairs, and attempted to embrace Mr. Redhead. Then the fun grew fast and furious. Some of the more riotous pushed the soot-covered chimney-sweeper against Mr. Redhead, as he tried to escape. They threw both him and his tormentor down on the ground in the churchyard where the soot-bag had been emptied, and though, at last, Mr. Redhead escaped into the "Black Bull," the doors of which were immediately barred, the people raged without, threatening to stone him and his friends.' [1] They escaped from the place, and Mr. Redhead, completely vanquished, retired from the curacy of Haworth.

Mr. Brontë, who had made a favourable impression on the inhabitants, was now accepted by them, and the natural kindness of his disposition and the urbanity of his manners, secured peace and contentment in the village.

His responsibilities as a pastor were not light, though the new scene of his labours, in moral condition, was, perhaps, no worse than the generality of similar villages in the north of England. The special chroniclers of Haworth speak of the population of the barren mountains west of York as 'rude and arrogant, after the manner of their wild country.' This is the testimony of James Rither, a Yorkshire esquire. The celebrated Oliver Haywood, preaching at the house of Jonas Foster, at Haworth, on June 13th, 1672, broke out into lamentations about the immorality, corruption, and profanity of the place. Mr. Grimshaw, in the last century, while curate there, had a conviction that the majority of the people were going to hell with their eyes open! Mrs. Gaskell informs us that at Haworth, 'drinking without the head being affected was considered a manly accomplishment.' A remarkable instance of the loss of reverence and the increase of profanity, in those days, is found in the observance of Palm Sunday at Heptonstall, a neighbouring village, and at Haworth itself this feast was pre-eminently distinguished in ancient times by the out-door processions of people going from the church and returning to it, bearing palm branches and singing the psalms and hymns appointed for the special festival.

It is known, indeed, that this feast was attended by the inhabitants of the surrounding hills and valleys in those times; and, at the period of which I speak, the attendance of the people was not diminished, but increased, though they came for another object. It is a singular fact that local feuds, if we may call them such, were kept up between the villages of the West Riding. And thus challenges were given alternately by Haworth to Heptonstall, and by Heptonstall to Haworth, for struggles between the champions of the respective villages, to be fought out on Palm Sunday. The inhabitants of these places, therefore, met to pound and pummel each other without any civil or religious cause to give bitterness to the fray: greed of triumph and brutal indifference to injuries inflicted characterized these hostile meetings. On such occasions, at Heptonstall, amidst great drunkenness and rioting, there were 'stand-up' fights from the church-gates to the 'Buttress,' a steep part of the road, near the bridge which crosses the river at the foot of Heptonstall Bank—nearly a mile in extent. On one of these feasts, a Haworth belligerent, unwilling to return home, although night was drawing on, and looking extremely dissatisfied, when asked by his wife what ailed him, answered, 'Aw 'annot fawhten wi' onny body yet, an' aw'll nut gooa whom till aw dun summat.' His affectionate spouse replied, 'Then gooa, an' get fawhten' an' ha' done wi' it, for we mun gooa.' The West-Riding police, on their institution, put an end to these disagraceful proceedings.

Haworth, the new place of Mr. Brontë's incumbency, which has been well and very fully described by many writers, is situated on the western confines of the parish of Bradford, and stands on a somewhat lofty eminence. It is, however, protected in great measure from the western storms by still higher ground, which consists of irreclaimable moors and morasses.

The church in which he, for the remainder of his life, performed his religious services, and in which his more gifted children repose, after their brief but memorable lives, was of ancient date. A chantry was founded there at the beginning of the reign of Edward III., where a priest celebrated daily for the repose of the soul of Adam de Battley, and for the souls of his ancestors, and for all the faithful departed. The church, which is dedicated to the glory of God, in honour of St. Michael the archangel, has been recently, to a great extent, re-edified. The old structure retained traces of one still older, of the early English style. Invested as it was with the evidences of the periods of taste good and bad through which it had passed, and with the associations which attach to old and familiar internal arrangements, it was endeared to the inhabitants. Of such associations the present church—though an architectural gain upon its predecessor—is necessarily destitute, and the world-wide interest with which the former structure was invested through the genius of the Brontës has been almost destroyed by the substitution of an edifice in which they never prayed, and which they never saw; though their remains repose, it is true, under its pavement, as is indicated by memorial tablets.

During the existence of the old church, Haworth was visited by continuous streams of people; but, on its removal, little was left to attract pilgrims from afar, and there was a manifest diminution of visitors to the village.

In the recent alterations, the parsonage also, in which the children of the Rev. Patrick Brontë lived and won for themselves enduring fame in the path of literature, has undergone considerable changes. It has been found necessary to add a new wing to the house, in order to obtain larger accommodation, and, to beautify the parsonage still further, the old cottage panes, through which light fell on precious and invaluable pages of elaborate manuscript, as they passed through delicate and gifted hands, have given way to plate-glass squares. Altogether the house, both inside and out, presents a very different appearance from that which it did in the time of the Brontës.

The chapelry at Haworth, when Mr. Brontë accepted the perpetual curacy, was much more populous and important than that of Thornton. The stipend of £170 per annum, with a fair residence attached, and a sum of £27 13s. for maintenance, made the change a desirable one on pecuniary grounds; and, with Mrs. Brontë's annuity of £50 a year, anxiety on this head was no doubt allayed.

The population of the district was about four thousand seven hundred, and, in the first ten years of Mr. Brontë's incumbency, increased by nearly twelve hundred souls. The chapelry included within its bounds the townships or hamlets of Stanbury and Near and Far Oxenhope, with the extensive moors and scattered houses stretching to the borders of Lancashire. The curacy of Stanbury, a place one mile west of Haworth, with £100 per annum, was in the gift of Mr. Brontë; and there was also the interest on £600, with a house, for the maintenance of a free school at that place, and a sum of £90 per annum for a like purpose at Haworth. In the year 1849, while Mr. Brontë was still incumbent, the chapelry of Haworth was divided, a church having been erected at Oxenhope at a cost of £1,500, the curacy there being valued at £150 per annum.

Among the considerations which had weight with Mr. Brontë in his determination to accept the curacy of Haworth was, in all probability, the delicate state of his wife's health, and the not over-robust constitutions of his children. He knew, that though from the smoke-laden atmosphere of the busy centres of West-

Riding industry, Keighley and Haworth were not wholly exempt, yet the winds which prevailed from the west and the south-west for a great part of the year, and swept over the moorlands from whose heights the Irish Channel itself was visible, would, by their purity, give that invigoration of which his family stood in need. It is quite possible, indeed, that by Mr. Brontë's removal to Haworth, which gave an almost illimitable range of wild, heathery hills for his children to wander over, an extension of their short lives may have been attained. Mrs. Brontë, however, derived little or no benefit from the change. She had suffered for some time under a fatal malady—an internal cancer—of which, about eighteen months after her arrival at Haworth, she died.

CHAPTER II.

MRS. BRONTË.

The Mother of the Brontës—Character and Personal Appearance —Literary Taste—, her Native Place—of Penzance—Branwell Family—Traits of Maria Branwell — Virtues—Letters to Mr. Brontë—Domestic Experiences.

The mother of the Brontës—whose death, in September, 1821, deprived her children of the affectionate and tender care which, for the short period of her married life, she had bestowed upon them—would, had she been spared, have moulded their characters by her own meek, gentle, and maternal virtues. Mrs. Brontë is said to have been small in person, but of graceful and kindly manners; not beautiful, yet comely and lady-like, and gifted with great discrimination, judgment, and modesty. Mrs. Gaskell says she 'was very elegant, and always dressed with a quiet simplicity of taste which accorded well with her general character, and of which some details call to mind the style of dress preferred by her daughter for her favourite heroines.' Mrs. Brontë was also gifted with literary ability and taste. She had written an essay entitled, 'The Advantages of Poverty in Religious Concerns,' with a view to publication in some periodical; and her letters were characterized by elegance and ease. Her relations in Penzance spoke of her as 'their favourite aunt, and one to whom they, as well as the family, looked up as a person of talent and great amiability of disposition;' and again, as 'possessing more than ordinary talents, which she inherited from her father.'

Mrs. Brontë, as has been said, was a native of Penzance, a

corporate town in the county of Cornwall, and also a sea-port. Penzance is situated in the hundred of Penwith, and is the most westerly town in England. The climate is distinguished by great mildness and salubrity, and the land is remarkable for its fertility, and the beauty of its meads and pastures. Its maritime situation, however, had, in former times, exposed it to the descents of foreign invaders, the last of which appears to have been that of the Spaniards in the year 1595. The account given of this event is that the invaders, being masters of Bretagne, sent four vessels manned with a force sufficient to occupy the Cornish coast. They landed near Mousehole—a well-known place on the western side of Mount's Bay—and entered the town, which they set on fire, the inhabitants fleeing before them. At a later date the town became very pleasant, and many of the houses were large and respectable, while the streets were well paved. Generally the people enjoyed long lives, and some attained the patriarchal age: one of these— Dolly Pentreath, who died in her one hundred and second year, and who had made the 'Mousehole' her residence—was known as the last who spoke Cornish. On account of the gentleness of the climate, many suffering from pulmonary complaints took up their residence there.

Penzance was a town surrounded by places of great interest to the historian and the antiquary, which are fully described by Borlase and others. The trades carried on at the place were of considerable extent in tin and the pilchard fishery, as well as in copper, earthenware, clay, and in other objects of manufacture and merchandise. In one of the local industries, Mr. Thomas Branwell was engaged. He had married a lady named Carne, and they had four daughters and one son. Maria was their third daughter. The families of Mr. and Mrs. Branwell were well connected, and moved in the best society in Penzance. They were Wesleyan Methodist in religion, and the children were brought up in that persuasion. Mr. Branwell relieved the cares of business by the delights and consolations of music, in the performance of which he is said to have had considerable ability. He and his wife lived to see their children grown up; and died, Mr. Branwell in 1808, and his wife in 1809.

Maria Branwell visited her uncle, Mr. Fennel, at the beginning of the summer of 1812, as is stated above, and, for the first time, saw Mr. Brontë. A feeling of mutual admiration sprang up between them, and something like the beginning of an engagement took place. When she returned home, a correspondence opened between the two, and Mr. Brontë preserved the letters. These have been referred to by the biographer of his daughter, and we learn that the communications of Miss Branwell were characterized by singular modesty, thoughtfulness, and piety. She was surprised to find herself so suddenly engaged, but she accepted with modest candour the proffer of Mr. Brontë's affection. The future was determined by mutual acquiescence. On Miss Branwell, nature had bestowed no great personal attractions, yet, as has been said, she was comely, and lady-like in her manners; and her innate grace drew irresistibly to her the esteem of all her acquaintants. Little is known respecting her beyond the personal traits already mentioned; and as to the circumstances and events of her life, unmarried or married, which was one of an extremely even and uneventful kind, little or nothing can be recorded beyond the ordinary routine of domestic duties well and affectionately performed, and of obligations in her sphere religiously observed. Blameless in her conduct, loving in her charge, and patient in the sufferings she was called upon to endure, she was a pattern of those excellencies which are the adornments of domestic life, and make the hearth happy and contented. It cannot be doubted that she ordered her household with judgment, and expended her husband's income with frugality and to the best advantage.

Mrs. Gaskell was enabled to give an extract from one of her letters written to Mr. Brontë before her marriage, which displays in an excellent manner her calm sensibility and understanding. She says: 'For some years I have been perfectly my own mistress, subject to no control whatever; so far from it that my sisters, who are many years older than myself, and even my dear mother, used to consult me on every occasion of importance, and scarcely ever doubted the propriety of my opinions and actions; perhaps you will be ready to accuse me of vanity in mentioning this, but you must consider that I do not boast of it. I have many times felt it a disadvantage, and although, I thank God, it has never led me into error, yet, in circumstances of uncertainty and doubt, I have deeply felt the want of a guide and instructor.' [2]

The usual preparations, which Mrs. Gaskell has particularized, were made for the wedding; but during the arrangements a disaster happened, to which the following letter to Mr. Brontë refers:—

'I suppose you never expected to be much richer for me, but I am sorry to inform you that I am still poorer than I thought myself. I mentioned having sent for my books, clothes, &c. On Saturday evening, about the time when you were writing the description of your imaginary shipwreck, I was reading and feeling the effects of a real one, having then received a letter from my sister, giving me an account of the vessel in which she had sent my box being stranded on the coast of Devonshire, in consequence of which the box was dashed to pieces with the violence of the sea, and all my little property, with the exception of a few articles, being swallowed up in the mighty deep. If this should not prove the prelude to something worse, I shall think little of it, as it is the first disastrous circumstance which has occurred since I left home.' [3]

The wedding took place at Guiseley, on December 29th, 1812, as is stated in the previous chapter.

CHAPTER III.

THE REV. PATRICK BRONTË.

Character of the Rev. P. Brontë—Charges against Him—
Allegations of Biographers—of the Charges—. Brontë's
indignant Denial of the Imputations—of Nancy Garrs—.
Brontë and the Silk-Dress Episode—. Brontë, the Supposed
Prototype of Mr. Helstone—Pistol-shots Theory—. Brontë
on Science Knowledge—Branwell.

The character of the Rev. Patrick Brontë, who was responsible,
after the death of his wife, for the education of his children,
if we may believe the accounts given of it by those who have
admired their genius, had many deplorable peculiarities. It
would be difficult, indeed, to find anywhere the record of such
passionate outbreaks, such unreasoning prejudices, and such
unbending will as are revealed in the stories which are told of
him. But we shall see presently that most of these charges have
no foundation in fact, while others are, probably, the result of
total misconception.

Mrs. Gaskell gives an account of these peculiarities. On one
occasion, she tells us, after the children had been out on the wet
moors, the nurse had rummaged out certain coloured boots
given to them by the Rev. Mr. Morgan, who had been sponsor
for Maria at Hartshead, and had arranged them before the fire.
Mr. Brontë observing this, and thinking the bright colours
might foster pride, heaped the boots upon the coals, and filled
the house with a very strong odour of burnt leather. 'Long before
this,' she says, 'some one had given Mrs. Brontë a silk gown

.... she kept it treasured up in her drawers. One day, however, while in the kitchen, she remembered that she had left the key in the drawer, and, hearing Mr. Brontë upstairs, she augured some ill to her dress, and, running up in haste, she found it cut into shreds.... He did not speak when he was annoyed or displeased, but worked off his volcanic wrath by firing pistols out of the back-door in rapid succession.... Now and then his anger took a different form, but still was speechless. Once he got the hearth-rug, and, stuffing it up the grate, deliberately set it on fire, and remained in the room in spite of the stench until it had smouldered and shrivelled away into uselessness. Another time he took some chairs, and sawed away at the backs till they were reduced to the condition of stools.' [4]

Mr. Wemyss Reid, who implicitly adopts the 'pistol shots' and 'pretty dress' stories, while paying a high tribute to Mr. Brontë's rectitude, and to his just pride in the celebrity of his daughters, says of him, 'He appears to have been a strange compound of good and evil. That he was not without some good is acknowledged by all who knew him. He had kindly feelings towards most people.... But throughout his whole life there was but one person with whom he had any real sympathy, and that person was himself.' He was 'passionate, self-willed, vain, habitually cold and distant in his demeanour towards those of his own household.' His wife 'lived in habitual dread of her lordly master.... It would be a mistake to suppose that violence was one of the weapons to which Mr. Brontë habitually resorted ... his general policy was to secure his end by craft rather than by force.' [5]

Miss Robinson, without hesitation, repeats the censures on Mr. Brontë published by Mrs. Gaskell and Mr. Reid, asking, 'Who dare say if that marriage was happy? Mrs. Gaskell, writing in the life and for the eyes of Mr. Brontë, speaks of his unwearied care, his devotion in the night-nursing. But, before that fatal illness was declared, she lets fall many a hint of the young wife's loneliness ... of her patient suffering, of his violent temper.' [6]

It will thus be seen that the disposition of Mr. Brontë must have been a sad one indeed, if all these statements are true; and marvellous that, with 'such a father,' the young and sterling faculties of the 'six small children' should have been so admirably directed and trained that, of the four who lived to later years, three at least occupy an exalted and prominent position among women of letters in the present century. And it would be still more strange that these children were especially distinguished for the gentleness of their dispositions, and the refinement of their ideas. It may be hoped that the readers of this volume, with their additional knowledge of the affectionate, but often wayward, Branwell, will sympathize with the sentiment which Monsieur Héger expressed in his letter to Mr. Brontë, that, *en jugeant un père de famille par ses enfants on ne risque pas de se tromper.* For we can scarcely doubt that the characteristics of the children, which I have named, were due, in fact, in great measure, to Mr. Brontë's affectionate supervision and education of them. He had graduated at St. John's College, Cambridge, as we have seen; and the culture and tone of the university were brought under the roof of his house, where his children—more especially Branwell—were subjected to its influence. Moreover, whatever may be thought of Mr. Brontë's intellectual gifts, or of the talent he displayed in his poems and prose writings, we may be sure that he possessed, in a marked degree, a deep sympathy with a higher mental training, and with the truth and simplicity of a pastoral life.

After the allegations against Mr. Brontë had appeared in the first edition of the life of his daughter Charlotte, he never ceased to deny the scandalous reflections upon his character in that work. 'They were,' he said to me, 'wholly untrue.' He stated that he had 'fulfilled every duty of a husband and a father with all the kindness, solicitude, and affection which could be required of him.' And Mrs. Brontë herself had said, as quoted by Mrs. Gaskell, 'Ought I not to be thankful that he never gave me an angry word?' thus openly declaring that, whatever might have been the peculiarities of Mr. Brontë's temper, his wife, at least, never suffered the consequences. The children also ever looked up to their father with reverence, gratitude, and devotion.

In a conversation I had with Mr. Brontë on the 8th of July, 1857, he spoke of the unjustifiable reflections upon himself which had been made public, and he said, 'I did not know that I had an enemy in the world, much less one who would traduce me before my death, till Mrs. Gaskell's "Life of Charlotte" appeared. Every thing in that book which relates to my conduct to my family is either false or distorted. I never did commit such acts as are there ascribed to me.' At a later interview Mr. Brontë explained that by the word 'enemies,' he implied, 'false informants and hostile critics.' He believed that Mrs. Gaskell had listened to village scandal, and had sought information from some discarded servant.

Let us then examine the source of these allegations. Mrs. Gaskell tells us that her informant was 'a good old woman,' who had been Mrs. Brontë's nurse in her illness. Now it is known that, whatever good qualities this person may be supposed to have had, her conscientiousness and rectitude, at least, were not of the first order, and she was detected in proceedings which caused Mr. Brontë to dismiss her at once. With the double effect of explaining her dismissal and injuring Mr. Brontë, this person gave an account of his temper and conduct, embellished with the stories which I have quoted from the first edition of the 'Life of Charlotte,' to a minister of the place; and it was in this way that Mrs. Gaskell became acquainted with her and them. Nancy Garrs, a faithful young woman who had been in Mr. Brontë's service at Thornton, who continued with the family after the removal to Haworth, and who still survives—a widow, Mrs. Wainwright—at an advanced age, a well-known inhabitant of Bradford, informs me that the 'silk dress' which Mr. Brontë is said to have torn to shreds was a print dress, not new, and that Mr. Brontë, disliking its enormous sleeves, one day, finding the opportunity, cut them off. The whole thing was a joke, which Mrs. Brontë at once guessed at, and, going upstairs, she brought the dress down, saying to Nancy, 'Look what he has done; that falls to your share.' Nancy declares the other stories to be wholly unfounded. She speaks of Mr. Brontë as a 'most affectionate husband; there never was a more affectionate father, never a kinder master;' and 'he was not of a violent temper at all; quite the reverse.'

This view of these slanderous stories is fortunately also confirmed out of the mouth of Charlotte Brontë. In the fourth chapter of 'Shirley,' speaking of Mr. Helstone—whose character, though not absolutely founded on that of her father, is yet unquestionably influenced by her knowledge of his disposition, and of some incidents in which he had been concerned,— she says that on the death of his wife, 'his dry-eyed and sober mourning scandalized an old housekeeper, and likewise a female attendant who had waited upon Mrs. Helstone in her sickness ... they gossiped together over the corpse, related anecdotes with embellishments of her lingering decline, and its real or supposed cause; in short, they worked each other up to some indignation against the austere little man, who sat examining papers in an adjoining room, unconscious of what opprobrium he was the object. Mrs. Helstone was hardly under the sod when rumours began to be rife in the neighbourhood that she had died of a broken heart; these magnified quickly into reports of hard usage, and, finally, details of harsh treatment on the part of her husband: reports grossly untrue, but not less eagerly received on that account.' It will thus be seen that the character of Mr. Helstone becomes in part a defence of Mr. Brontë. On the occasion above referred to, Mr. Brontë went on to say that, 'while duly acknowledging the obligations he felt himself under to Mrs. Gaskell for her admirable memoir of his daughter, he could not but regard her uncalled-for allusions to himself, and the failings of his son Branwell, as the excrescences of a work otherwise ably carried out.' He appeared, on this occasion, to be consoled by the thought that, owing to the remonstrances he had made, the objectionable passages would be expunged from the subsequent editions of the work, and that he would ultimately be set right with the public. He concluded with these words:—'I have long been an abstraction to the world, and it is not consoling now to be thus dragged before the public; to be represented as an unkind husband, and charged with acts which I never committed.'

The story of the pistol-shots admits of ready explanation. It is known that Mr. Brontë, like Helstone, had a strange fascination in military affairs, and he seems to have had almost the spirit of Uncle Toby. He lived, too, in the troublous times of the Luddites, and had kept pistols, for defence as Mr. Helstone did. That gentleman, it will be remembered, had two pairs suspended over the mantel-piece of his study, in cloth cases, kept loaded. As I have reason to know, Mr. Brontë, having been accustomed to the use of fire-arms, retained the possession of them for safety in the night; but, fearing they might become dangerous, occasionally discharged them in the day-time.

Mr. Brontë's remonstrances and denials, and his refutation of the scandals attributed to him, had their effect; and the charges complained of were entirely omitted in the edition of the 'Life of Charlotte,' published in the year 1860. Mr. Brontë was in his eighty-fourth year when this tardy act of bare justice was done to him. It may be added that the people of Haworth, when they saw in print Mrs. Gaskell's exaggerated and erroneous statements, loudly expressed their disapprobation. Mr. Wood, late churchwarden of Haworth, also denied the stories of the cutting up of Mrs. Brontë's dress, and the other charges just referred to.

The truth about Mr. Brontë appears to be this: that though, like Mr. Helstone—many of the *traits* of whose character were derived from that of the incumbent of Haworth—he might have missed his vocation, like him he was 'not diabolical at all,' and that, like him, also, 'he was a conscientious, hard-headed, hard-handed, brave, stern, implacable, faithful little man: a man almost without sympathy, ungentle, prejudiced, and rigid: but a man true to principle—honourable, sagacious, and sincere.' Possibly we should not be wholly mistaken in saying that, like the parson in 'Shirley,' Nature never intended him 'to make a very good husband, especially to a quiet wife.' He lacked the fine sympathy and delicate perception that would have enabled him to make his family entirely happy; and when brooding over his politics, his pamphlets, and his sermons, like Mr. Helstone, he probably locked 'his liveliness in his book-case and study-desk.' Yet Mr. Helstone is neither brutal nor insane, 'neither tyrannical nor hypocritical,' but 'simply a man who is rather liberal than good-natured, rather brilliant than genial, rather scrupulously equitable than truly just—if you can understand such superfine distinctions?'

It would not have been necessary, in this work, to defend at such length the character of the Rev. Patrick Brontë, had it not happened, unfortunately, that recent works, which have treated admirably of the writings of his daughters, have also acquiesced in, and to a great extent reiterated, the serious charges made against him. Moreover, it can never be a useless thing to retrieve a character which has been thoughtlessly taken away. This defence has now been made, and it may be hoped that the 'six motherless children' had a more amiable and affectionate father than is generally supposed, and that he paid careful and anxious attention to their bringing-up and to their education. Indeed, of this there need be no doubt. The death of his wife had placed them in his hands, he being their only support on earth, and it surely is not too much to say that he knew his duty, and did it well, as the lives of his children prove, on the ground of natural affection, and, perhaps, of higher motives also.

The following extract from a letter written by Mr. Brontë a few years later, in reference to scientific knowledge, is sufficiently characteristic. He says: 'In this age of innovation and scepticism, it is the incumbent duty of every man of an enlarged and pious mind to promote, to the utmost extent of his abilities, every movement in the variegated, complex system of human affairs, which may have either a direct, indirect, or collateral tendency to purify and expand the naturally polluted and circumscribed mind of fallen nature, and to raise it to that elevation which the Scriptures require, as well as the best interests of humanity.'

Upon the death of his wife, Mr. Brontë felt the need of some one to superintend the affairs of his household, and assist him in this important charge of the bringing-up of his children; and so, towards the end of the year 1822, an elder sister of the deceased lady, Miss Elizabeth Branwell of Penzance, came to reside with him. She is represented to have been, in personal appearance, of low and slight proportions; prim and starched in her attire, which was, when prepared for the reception of visitors, invariably of silk; and she wore, according to the fashion of the time, a frontal of auburn curls, gracefully overshadowing her forehead. She took occasionally, through habit, a pinch from her gold snuff-box, which she had always at hand. When she had taken up her residence at bleak, wild, and barren Haworth, she is said to have sighed for the flower-decked meads of sunny Penzance, her native place. Miss Branwell's affectionate regard for her dead sister's children caused her to take deep interest in everything relating to them, their health, the comfort and cleanliness of their home, and the sedulous culture of their minds. In the management of Mr. Brontë's household she was materially assisted by the faithful and trustworthy Tabby, who, in 1825, was added to the family as a domestic servant. By a long and faithful service of some thirty years in the Brontë family, Tabby gained the respect and confidence of the household. She had been born and nurtured in the chapelry of Haworth, at a time when mills and machinery were not, when railways had not made the inhabitants of the hills and valleys familiar with the cities and towns of England; and, moreover, before the ancient dialect, so interesting philologically to the readers of King Alfred's translations of Orosius and Bede, and the like, came to be considered rude, vulgar, and barbarous. Tabby used the dialect rightly, without any attempt to improve on the language of her childhood and of her fathers; and she was original and truthful in this, as in all her ways. It was from Tabby, principally, that the youthful Brontës gained the familiarity with the Yorkshire Doric, which they afterwards reproduced with such accuracy in 'Shirley,' 'Wuthering Heights,' and others of their writings.

CHAPTER IV.

THE GIRLHOOD OF THE BRONTË SISTERS.

Girlhood—of Character—'s Description of the Elf-land of
Childhood—Still and Solemn Moors of Haworth influence
their Writings—Present of Toys—Plays which they Acted—.
Brontë on a Supposed Earthquake—Evidence of his Care
for his Children—School at Haworth—Children under
the Tuition of the Master—Character of the School—
Bridge School—Charlotte's View of Mr. Carus Wilson's
Management—of Maria and Elizabeth.

The childhood of the Brontës in the parsonage of Haworth
has been pictured to us as a very strange one indeed. We have
seen them deprived in their early youth of that maternal care
which they required so much, and left in the hands of a father
unfamiliar with such a charge, who was filled with Spartan ideas
of discipline, and with theories of education above and beyond
the capacity of childhood. There was probably little room in the
house of Mr. Brontë for gaiety and amusement, very little tolerance
for pretty dress, or home beauty, and small comprehension of
childish needs. Rigid formality, silent chambers, staid attire,
frugal fare, and secluded lives fell to the lot of these thoughtful
and gifted children. It was no wonder that they grew up 'grave
and silent beyond their years;' that, when infantine relaxation
failed them, they betook themselves to reading newspapers, and
debating the merits of Hannibal and Cæsar, of Buonaparte and
Wellington; or that, when they were deprived of the company of
the village children by the '*Quis ego et quis tu?*' which was forced

too early upon them, they fled for silent companionship with the moors. Yet this childhood, stern and grim though it was, where we look in vain for the beautiful simplicity and sunny gladness which should ever distinguish the features of youth, had a beauty and a joy of its own; and it had a merit also. Charlotte Brontë herself has left us one of the most beautiful pictures which can be found in English literature of the pleasures of childhood, that elf-land which is passed before the shores of Reality have arisen in front; when they stand afar off, so blue, soft, and gentle that we long to reach them; when we 'catch glimpses of silver lines, and imagine the roll of living waters,' heedless of 'many a wilderness, and often of the flood of Death, or some stream of sorrow as cold and almost as black as Death' that must be crossed ere true bliss can be tasted. So the Brontës, trooping abroad on the moors, revelling in the freedom of Nature, while their faculties expanded to the noblest ends, lived also in the heroic world of childhood, 'its inhabitants half-divine or semi-demon; its scenes dream-scenes; darker woods and stranger hills; brighter skies, more dangerous waters; sweeter flowers, more tempting fruits; wider plains; drearier deserts; sunnier fields than are found in Nature.' Can we doubt that the Brontë children, endowed, as the world was afterwards to know, with keener perceptions, more exalted sympathies, and nobler gifts than other children, enjoyed these things more than others could? And the merit of their childhood was this: that it impressed them in the strongest form with the influence of locality, with the boundless expanse of the moors, and with the weird and rugged character of the people amongst whom they lived, and whom they afterwards drew so well. Such influences as these are a quality more or less traceable in the works of every author, but they are very apparent in the productions of the Brontës. These writers could not have produced 'Jane Eyre,' 'Shirley,' and 'Wuthering Heights' without them, any more than Goldsmith could have written his 'Vicar of Wakefield' if his early years had not been passed in the pleasant village of Lissey. The moors, clothed with purple heather and golden gorse in billowy waves, were certainly all in all to Emily Brontë; and she and her sisters, and the youthful Branwell with his ready admiration and brilliant fancy, escorted by Tabby, enjoyed to the full the free atmosphere of the heights around Haworth. The rushing sound of their own waterfall, and the shrill cries of the grouse, which flew up as they came along, were to them friendly voices of the opening life of Nature whose potent influence inspired them so well.

Of other companionship in their early years they had hardly any; and being unable to associate much with children of their own age and condition, or to play with their young and immediate neighbours in childish games, Mr. Brontë's son and daughters grew up amongst their elders with heads older than their years, and spoke with a knowledge that might have sprung from actual experience of men and manners. They were, in fact, 'old-fashioned children.' Their extraordinary cleverness was soon observed, and the servants were always on their guard lest any of their remarks might be repeated by the children. Notwithstanding this, the little Brontës were children still, and took pleasure in the things of childhood. Up-grown men will not whip a top on the causeways, nor trundle a hoop through the streets, nor play at 'hide-and-seek' at dusk as of yore; but the Brontë children in their youthful days did all these things, and they entered at times with ardour, despite their precocious gravity, into the simple joys and amusements of childhood, as is testified by the eager delight with which they regarded the presents of the toys they received.

The earliest notice we have of Branwell Brontë is that Charlotte remembered having seen her mother playing with him during one golden sunset in the parlour of the parsonage at Haworth. Later, we are informed that Mr. Brontë brought from Leeds on one occasion a box of wooden soldiers for him. The children were in bed, but the 'next morning,' says Charlotte, in one of her juvenile manuscripts, 'Branwell came to our door with a box of soldiers. Emily and I jumped out of bed, and I snatched up one and exclaimed, "This is the Duke of Wellington! This shall be the duke!" When I had said this, Emily likewise took up one and said it should be hers; when Anne came down she said one should be hers. Mine was the prettiest of the whole, and the tallest, and the most perfect in every part. Emily's was a grave-looking fellow, and we called him "Gravey." Anne's was a queer little thing much like herself, and we called him "Waiting-boy." Branwell chose his, and called him "Buonaparte." So Charlotte relates these glad incidents of their childhood with pleasure, and places on record the joy they inspired.

Mr. Brontë says, 'When mere children, as soon as they could read and write, Charlotte and her brother and sisters used to invent and act little plays of their own, in which the Duke of Wellington, my daughter Charlotte's hero, was sure to come off conqueror; when a dispute would not infrequently arise amongst them regarding the comparative merits of Buonaparte, Hannibal, and Cæsar.'

In acting their early plays, they performed them with childish glee, and did not fail at times to 'tear a passion to tatters.' They observed that Tabby did not approve of such extraordinary proceedings; but on one occasion, with increased energy of action and voice, they so wrought on her fears that she retreated to her nephew's house, and, as soon as she could regain her breath, she exclaimed, 'William! yah mun gooa up to Mr. Brontë's, for aw'm sure yon childer's all gooin mad, and aw darn't stop 'ith hause ony longer wi' 'em; an' aw'll stay here woll yah come back!' When the nephew reached the parsonage, 'the childer set up a great crack o' laughin',' at the wonderful joke they had perpetrated on faithful Tabby.

Mr. Brontë—like other parents and friends of precocious and gifted children, who, in after-life have become celebrated in religion, art, poetry, literature, politics, or war, and who have given out in childhood tokens of brilliant and sterling gifts which have been recorded in their biographies—saw in his own children evidences of that mental power, fervid imagination, and superior faculty of language and expression, which were developed in them in after-years. He often fancied that great powers lay in his children, and it cannot be doubted that he sometimes looked forward to and hoped for a brilliant future for his offspring. It was this hope that cheered him, and he gave to Mrs. Gaskell, for publication, all the evidences of genius in his son and daughters, as children, which he could remember. But, from the information he imparted to that writer, we can scarcely gather, I fear, sufficient to justify the inference he drew, or appears to have drawn, for the particulars given border too much on the trivial and unimportant. Perhaps Mr. Brontë failed to remember the special evidences he had observed of what he intended to convey at the actual moment of communication. Be this as it may, no doubt remained on his mind that genius was apparent in his children above and apart from their eager reading of magazines and newspapers, nor that other schemes and objects occupied their thoughts than the interests and contentions of the political parties of the hour.

'When my children were very young,' says Mr. Brontë,—'when, as far as I can remember, the oldest was about ten years of age, and the youngest about four,—thinking that they knew more than I had yet discovered, in order to make them speak with less timidity, I deemed that, if they were put under a sort of cover, I might gain my end; and, happening to have a mask in the house, I told them all to stand and speak boldly from under cover of the mask. I began with the youngest (Anne, afterwards Acton Bell), and asked what a child like her most wanted; she answered, "Age and experience." I asked the next (Emily, afterwards Ellis Bell) what I had best do with her brother Branwell, who was sometimes a naughty boy; she answered, "Reason with him, and, when he won't listen to reason, whip him." I asked Branwell what was the best way of knowing the difference between the intellects of man and woman; he answered, "By considering the difference between them as to their bodies."' In answer to a question as to which were the two best books, Charlotte said that 'the Bible,' and after it the 'Book of Nature,' were the best. Mr. Brontë then asked the next daughter, 'What is the best mode of education for a woman;' she answered, 'That which would make her rule her house well.' He then asked the eldest, Maria, 'What is the best mode of spending time;' she answered, 'By laying it out in preparation for a happy eternity.' He says he may not have given the exact words, but they were nearly so, and they had made a lasting impression on his memory. [7]

But the intellectual pabulum of Mr. Brontë's children, for some time, consisted, for the most part, as we are told, of magazines and newspapers. As these took the place of toy-books and fairy tales, their young minds were attracted by such moral subjects and entertaining stories as were treated of in the serials of the day; and their attention was also largely engaged in the political questions which were then debated in the Houses of Parliament. Imbibing from their father their religious and political views and opinions, they became strong partizans and supporters of the leading Conservatives in the House of Lords and the House of Commons. They had often heard conversations between their father and aunt on these subjects; they listened with interested attention, and obtained information as to the outer world and its pursuits. By their surroundings their minds were soon raised above the thoughts, desires, and interests of childhood in general; and, under the circumstances, though it may seem odd, it is not extraordinary that wooden soldiers should thus be made, by these talented children, to represent the two great opposing warriors of the present age.

In addition to the general bringing-up of his children at home, and the formal tasks which Mr. Brontë set them, magazines and other publications were thrown about, and Maria, being the eldest, was wont to read the newspapers when she was less than nine years old, and reported matters of home and foreign interest, as well as those relating to the public characters and current affairs of the day, to her young brother and sisters. Indeed, so earnest was her relevancy on such occasions in these unchildish and grave questions, that she could talk upon them with discriminating intelligence to her father, whose interest in his children thus grew, as their faculties expanded. The young Brontës, though still in childhood's years, were soon no longer children in intellect: they touched, in fact, the 'Shores of Reality' at an earlier age than most children; and, though interested sometimes, perhaps momentarily, in trivial matters, they seem to have turned almost everything to literary account. Even Branwell's toys, which they all received so gleefully, gave rise to the 'Young Men's Play.'

Mr. Brontë, though interested deeply in the gradual development of the mental gifts of his children, did not fail, after his wife's death, to promote and protect their health, and he availed himself of the means which the chapelry of Haworth afforded. For this object he encouraged recreation on the moors at suitable times, and subjected the young members of his family to the pure and exhilarating breeze that, redolent of heather, breathed over them from the sea, during the summer and autumnal months.

On Tuesday, September the 2nd, 1824, a severe thunderstorm, and an almost unprecedented downfall of rain which resembled, in volume, a waterspout, caused the irruption of an immense bog, at Crow Hill, an elevation, between Keighley and Colne, and about one thousand feet above the sea-level. The mud, mingled with stones, many of large size, rolled down a precipitous and rugged clough that descended from it. Reaching the hamlet of Pondens, the torrent expanded and overspread the corn-fields adjoining to the depth of several feet, with many other devastating consequences.

Mr. Brontë regarded this as the effect of an earthquake, and he sent a communication to the 'Leeds Mercury,' in which he says: 'At the time of the irruption, the clouds were copper-coloured, gloomy, and lowering, the atmosphere was strongly electrified, and unusually close.' In the same month—on Sunday, September 12th, 1824—he preached a sermon on the subject, in Haworth

Church, in which he informed his hearers that, the day of disaster being exceedingly fine, he had sent his little children, who were indisposed, accompanied by the servants, to take an airing on the common, and, as they stayed rather longer than he expected, he went to an upper chamber to look out for their return. The heavens over the moors were blackening fast; he heard the muttering of distant thunder, and saw the frequent flashes of lightning. Though, ten minutes before, there was scarcely a breath of air stirring, the gale freshened rapidly and carried along with it clouds of dust and stubble. 'My little family,' he continued, 'had escaped to a place of shelter, but I did not know it.' These were Charlotte, Branwell, Emily, and Anne. Their sisters, Maria and Elizabeth, were then at Cowan Bridge.

When Mr. Brontë accepted the living of Haworth, he had found existing there a Grammar School, and he took in it a special and personal interest, for it was an old institution, was endowed, and had recently been renovated. It was his policy to show that he took an interest in it; so that, by adding his support to that of the trustees, he might possibly confirm their favourable opinion of him, and secure their continued good feeling. This was essential at the time, as any appearance of coldness on his part towards their cherished foundation would have perhaps evoked a spirit akin to that which caused the compulsory resignation of Mr. Redhead, or have induced an estrangement between himself and the trustees. It is stated, with regard to this Grammar School, that one Christopher Scott by will, dated the 4th of October, 13th of Charles I., gave a school-house which he had built adjoining the church-way; and ordained that there should be a school-master who should be a graduate at least, a bachelor, if not a master of arts, and who should teach Greek and Latin. The school had been enlarged in 1818, when the Brontë family were still at Thornton, and a new house was then erected for the master by the trustees.

As this foundation was designed to provide a classical education for its students, it was one to which the better classes in the neighbourhood need not have hesitated to entrust their children for superior instruction than could possibly be had in the ordinary schools of the district. The school was situated close to the parsonage, a lane only intervening, and it was commodious and lightsome. But Mr. Brontë, on his arrival, found that it had not for some time been maintained as a regular Grammar School: that there was little or no demand for the advantages of a classical education for their children among the inhabitants of the chapelry. [8] Yet the master who received the appointment from the trustees at the Midsummer of 1826, although not even a graduate of either of the universities, was stated to be competent to teach Latin, and was a man of considerable attainments, instructing both boys and girls in every essential branch of knowledge. In this the tutor differed nothing from some of his immediate predecessors. But, though education of this sort was thus immediately at hand, Mr. Brontë does not appear to have availed himself of it for his daughters, or his son Branwell, for any great length of time. Mrs. Gaskell says, indeed, that their regular tasks were given by himself. Mr. Brontë, however, probably heard his children repeat early lessons set by the master in order to ascertain with what facility they had learned them. At a later date, Branwell and his sisters took a larger interest in the Grammar School, and they became active and willing teachers in the Sunday-school, which was connected with it. They were, indeed, often seen, as is yet remembered, in the processions of the scholars.

Although Mr. Brontë had taken vigilant and affectionate care to promote the health of his children, he was well aware that though he could strengthen their constitutions in some sort, delicate by nature as they were, he could not ward off with certainty the diseases and sufferings incident to childhood, from which his children were, indeed, unfortunately destined to suffer. Solicitude therefore came upon the parsonage when Maria and Elizabeth were attacked by measles and whooping-cough. Recovering partially from these attacks, it was thought desirable to send them—perhaps partly for change of air—to a school which had somewhat recently been established at Cowan Bridge, a hamlet on the coach-road between Leeds and Kendal, which was easily reached from Haworth, as the coach passed daily. This school was especially established for the board and education of the daughters of such clegymen of the Establishment as required it. It was begun, as we know from Mrs. Gaskell's 'Life of Charlotte Brontë,' by the Rev. William Carus Wilson; and we are aware also that severe and unqualified censures were passed upon its situation and management by the author of 'Jane Eyre,' in after-years, under the description of Lowood, and that the Ellen Burns of the story was no other than Maria Brontë. Readers of 'Jane Eyre' became indignant, and the Cowan Bridge School was execrated, denounced, and condemned by the public, to the utter distress and pain of its founder and patron.

In reference to this affair, Charlotte indeed said to her future biographer that 'she should not have written what she did of Lowood in "Jane Eyre" if she had thought the place would have been so immediately identified with Cowan Bridge, although there was not a word in her account of the institution but what was true at the time when she knew it. She also said that she had not considered it necessary in a work of fiction to state every particular with the impartiality that might be required in a court of justice, nor to seek out motives, and make allowances for human failings, as she might have done, if dispassionately analyzing the conduct of those who had the superintendence of the institution.' Mrs. Gaskell believes Charlotte 'herself would have been glad of an opportunity to correct the over strong impression which was made upon the public mind by her vivid picture, though even she, suffering her whole life long both in heart and body from the consequences of what happened there, might have been apt, to the last, to take her deep belief in facts for the facts themselves—her conception of truth for the absolute truth.' [9]

But it is only just to Mr. Wilson to say that the low situation of the premises fixed upon, the arrangement of the school-buildings, and the inefficient management of the domestic department, do not appear to have been so fatal to the boarders, even if we admit all the alleged severities of the regimen. For, when a low fever, or influenza cold, which was not regarded by Dr. Batty as 'either alarming or dangerous,' broke out at the school, and some forty of the pupils fell more or less under its influence, none died of it at Cowan Bridge, and only one, Mrs. Gaskell informs us, from after consequences at home; and, though delicate, the Brontë children entirely escaped the attack. Mrs. Gaskell has, however, entered at considerable length into a detailed account of the alleged mismanagement of the school, the severities exercised over the pupils—especially by one of the responsible tutors, 'Miss Scatcherd,'—the cooking and insufficiency of food, the general neglect of sanitary regulations in the domestic department, and the utter unfitness of the place itself for the continued health and comfort of the inmates. But the biographer of Charlotte Brontë in after-years considerably modified the severe strictures which her heroine had thought fit to describe in 'Jane Eyre,'—an admirable work of fiction, though not necessarily one of fact— and she says, speaking of Charlotte's account of the Cowan Bridge School: 'The pictures, ideas, and conceptions of character received into the mind of the child of eight years old were destined to be reproduced in fiery words a quarter of a century afterwards. She saw but one side of Mr. Wilson's character; and many of those who knew him at the time assure me of the fidelity with which this is represented, while at the same time they regret that the delineation should have obliterated, as it were, nearly all that was noble and conscientious.' It appears also that Mr. Wilson had 'grand and fine qualities'—which were left unnoticed by Charlotte—of which the biographer had received 'abundant evidence.' [10] Of these Mr. Brontë seems to have been aware, as Charlotte and Emily were sent back to Cowan Bridge after the deaths of Maria and Elizabeth. Mrs. Gaskell wonders Charlotte did not remonstrate against her father's decision to send her and Emily back to the place, knowing, as we may suppose she did, of the alleged infliction which her dead sisters had endured at the very school to which she and Emily were returning. Surely such a very miserable state of things as is described in 'Jane Eyre' could not have existed at the time to impress on Charlotte's mind such a dread as we are asked to believe she had, and Mr. Brontë could not be aware that any serious objections to the school existed. Indeed, the true condition of the institution at the period is apparent from the testimony of the noble and benevolent Miss Temple of 'Jane Eyre,' whose husband thus writes: 'Often have I heard my late dear wife speak of her sojourn at Cowan Bridge; always in terms of admiration of Mr. Carus Wilson, his parental love to his pupils, and their love for him; of the food and general treatment, in terms of approval. I have heard her allude to an unfortunate cook who used at times to spoil the porridge, but who, she said, was soon dismissed.'

While at Cowan Bridge, Maria's health had suddenly given way, and alarming symptoms declared themselves. Mr. Brontë was sent for. He had known nothing of her illness, and was terribly shocked when he saw her. He ascended the Leeds coach with his dying child. Mrs. Gaskell says, 'the girls crowded out into the road to follow her with their eyes, over the bridge, past the cottages, and then out of sight for ever.'

The poignancy of Mr. Brontë's grief on this occasion was profound, and all but insupportable. Here was his first-born, the early joy of his home at Hartshead, the intelligent and brilliantly gifted companion of the first few years of his widowed life— dying before him! She, whose innocent and thoughtful converse had cheered his solitary moments, and whose merry laugh had often made the hearth glad, whose affectionate care of her little brother and sisters, disinterested as it was incessant, supplied for them the offices of their deceased mother—was fading from his sight! Arriving at Haworth, they were received with sincere and tearful sympathy by Miss Branwell, and with childish alarm and dread by Branwell and Anne. Every care which affection could provide was bestowed on the sinking child, but she died, a few days after her arrival, on May 6, 1825.

Elizabeth, too, struck down with the same fatal disease, came home to die of consumption on June 15 in the same year, but a month and a few days after her sister. These sorrowful events were never forgotten by Branwell, and the impressions made upon his mind by the deaths and funeral rites he had witnessed became the theme of some of his later and more mournful effusions.

The early recollection of Maria at Cowan Bridge was that she was delicate, and unusually clever and thoughtful for her age. Of Elizabeth Miss Temple writes: 'The second, Elizabeth, is the only one of the family of whom I have a vivid recollection, from her meeting with a somewhat alarming accident; in consequence of which I had her for some days and nights in my bedroom, not only for the sake of greater quiet, but that I might watch over her myself…. Of the two younger ones (if two there were) I have very slight recollections, save that one, a darling child under five years of age, was quite the pet nursling of the school.'

'This last,' says Mrs. Gaskell, 'would be Emily. Charlotte was considered the most talkative of the sisters—a "bright, clever little child."' [11]

CHAPTER V.

BRANWELL'S BOYHOOD.

Reunion of the Brontë Family—is the supposed Prototype of Victor Crimsworth—Character not a complete Portrait of Branwell—Friendships—His Visit to the Keighley Feast—Effect on Branwell's Nerves—Wrestle—Lost Spectacles—of his Father's Displeasure—Mrs. Gaskell's Story of the 'Black Bull' Incident Questioned—Branwell and her Nephew.

Upon the return of Charlotte and Emily from Cowan Bridge, the youthful Brontës, whom death had spared, were united again; and, for some years more, followed their pursuits together, until Charlotte went to school at Roe Head in 1831. Branwell was the constant companion of his sisters during these childish years, and they all looked upon him with pride and affection. Charlotte, in those days, was a sympathetic friend to him; and, in his later years, he felt it a source of deep regret that she was somewhat estranged. But the gentle Emily—after the death of Maria—was his chief companion, and a warm affection never lost its ardour between them. The sisters were quick to perceive the Promethean spark that burned in their brother, and they looked upon Branwell, as indeed did all who knew him, as their own superior in mental gifts. In his childhood even, Branwell Brontë showed great aptitude for acquiring knowledge, and his perceptive powers were very marked. He was, too, gifted with a sprightly disposition, tinged at times with great melancholy, but he acquired early a lively and fascinating address. There was a fiery ardour and eagerness in his manner which told of his abundant animal spirits, and he entered with avidity into the enjoyments of the life that lay before him. Charlotte, who knew well the treasures of her brother's opening faculties, his ability, his learning, and his affection, saw also many things that alarmed her in his disposition. She saw the abnormal and unhealthy flashing of his intellect, and marked that weakness and want of self-control which left Branwell, when subjected to temptation, a prey to many destructive influences, whose effect shall hereafter be traced. There is reason to believe that Charlotte pictures this period of Branwell's life in 'The Professor,' where she describes the childhood of Victor Crimsworth; and, though the extract is rather long, it is given here as valuable, because it furnishes a full record of the early powers of Branwell, and of the manner in which his sister—by the light of subsequent events—looked upon them and upon his failings, and it will be seen that towards the latter she is somewhat inflexible.

'Victor,' she makes William Crimsworth say, 'is as little of a pretty child as I am of a handsome man ... he is pale and spare, with large eyes.... His shape is symmetrical enough, but slight.... I never saw a child smile less than he does, nor one who knits such a formidable brow when sitting over a book that interests him, or while listening to tales of adventure, peril, or wonder.... But, though still, he is not unhappy—though serious, not morose; he has a susceptibility to pleasurable sensations almost too keen, for it amounts to enthusiasm.... When he could read, he became a glutton of books, and is so still. His toys have been few, and he has never wanted more. For those he possesses he seems to have contracted a partiality amounting to affection; this feeling, directed towards one or two living animals of the house, strengthens almost to a passion.... I saw in the soil of his heart healthy and swelling germs of compassion, affection, fidelity. I discovered in the garden of his intellect a rich growth of wholesome principles—reason, justice, moral courage, promised, if not blighted, a fertile bearing.... She (his mother) sees, as I also see, a something in Victor's temper—a kind of electrical ardour and power—which emits, now and then, ominous sparks; Hunsden calls it his spirit, and says it should not be curbed. I call it the leaven of the offending Adam, and consider that it should be, if not *whipped* out of him, at least soundly disciplined; and that he will be cheap of any amount of either bodily or mental suffering which will ground him radically in the art of self-control. Frances (his mother) gives this *something* in her son's marked character no name; but when it appears in the grinding of his teeth, in the glittering of his eye, in the fierce revolt of feeling against disappointment, mischance, sudden sorrow, or supposed injustice, she folds him to her breast, or takes him to walk with her alone in the wood; then she reasons with him like any philosopher, and to reason Victor is ever accessible; then she looks at him with eyes of love, and by love Victor can be infallibly subjugated. But will reason or love be the weapons with which in future the world will meet his violence? Oh, no! for that flash in his black eye—for that cloud on his bony brow—for that compression of his statuesque lips, the lad will some day get blows instead of blandishments, kicks instead of kisses; then for the fit of mute fury which will sicken the body and madden his soul; then for the ordeal of merited and salutary suffering out of which he will come (I trust) a wiser and a better man.'

The natural adornments and defects of Branwell's mind in boyhood, which may to some extent be traced in Charlotte's picture of Victor Crimsworth, in 'The Professor,' must not be regarded otherwise than as possessing a general resemblance to those which are found in that character. Physically, Branwell and Crimsworth were dissimilar, though mentally there is a portraiture; but even here, Charlotte, having him in her mind when she sketched the character of Victor, exaggerated therein, as she had done in other instances, the actual defects of her brother. It is true, nevertheless, that those who knew Branwell Brontë in early life could see in him the original of Victor Crimsworth.

In the following pages the greatness of Branwell's genius may be observed,—great, though marred by the errors and misfortunes of his life,—as well as by the sorrows which his impulsive, kindly, and affectionate nature brought upon himself, sorrows thus sadly set forth by his sister as the outcome of his passions, and described by her as the penalty of his future years.

In Branwell Brontë, the 'leaven of the offending Adam' might now and then certainly be observed, but it was largely modified by the ameliorating influences of his home; and, although, from the failings common to humanity, the children of Mr. Brontë could not be free, his early waywardness and petulance were, by the influence of sex, more forcibly expressed than such failings could be in his sisters. Between the children of Mr. Brontë, however, there existed even more than the ordinary affections of childhood. At this period of their lives, they were ignorant of the wiles of corrupt human nature, and Branwell, with all the lightsome exuberance of his boyhood, returned without stint the ardent and deep affection of his sisters. But, when a few years had rolled on, he awoke to the sunny morning of youth; and, in the absence of a brother, sought companionship with certain youths of Haworth, and made them playmates. Amongst them was one, the brother of some friends of his sisters, who became to him a personal associate, and it was with this companion that he was wont to sport on the moors, across the meadows, and, with joyous laugh, along the streets of the village.

The survivor of these two friends gives me an incident that occurred at the time of the annual Feast at Keighley, which the youths visited. The town was, as is usual on such occasions, crowded with booths and shows, and various places of entertainment. Players and riders,—men and women,—clothed in gay raiments, rendered brilliant with spangles, paced backwards and forwards along their platforms to the sound of drums, organs, and Pandean pipes, cymbals, tambourines, and castanets. There were stalls, too, weighted with nuts and various confectionaries, and there were also rocking-boats and merry-go-rounds, with other amusements.

As the evening advanced, and the shows were lighted up,

Branwell's excitement, hilarity, and extravagance knew no bounds: he would see everything and try everything. Into a rocking-boat he and his friend gaily stepped. The rise of the boat, when it reached its full height, gave Branwell a pleasant view of the fair beneath; but, when it descended, he screamed out at the top of his voice, 'Oh! my nerves! my nerves! Oh! my nerves!' On each descent, every nerve thrilled, tingled, and vibrated with overwhelming effect through the overwrought and delicate frame of the boy. Leaving the fair, the two proceeded homeward; and, reaching a country spot, near a cottage standing among a thicket of trees, Branwell, still full of exuberant life, proposed a wrestle with his companion. They engaged in a struggle, when Branwell was overthrown. It was not until reaching the village, and seeing the lights in the windows, with considerably enlarged rays, that he became aware he had lost his spectacles,—for Branwell was, like his sister Charlotte, very near-sighted. This was, indeed, no little trouble to him, as he was in great fear lest his father should notice his being without them, and institute unpleasant inquiries as to what had become of them. He told his fears to his companion; but, after a sleepless night for both, Branwell's friend was early on the spot in search of the missing spectacles, when the woman living in the cottage close by, seeing a youth looking about, came to him, and, learning for what he sought, brought out the glasses which she had picked up from the ground just before he came. M——, glad of the discovery, hastened to the parsonage, which he reached to find Branwell astir, who was overjoyed on receiving the missing spectacles, as the danger of his father's displeasure was avoided.

Mrs. Gaskell has written an account of the brother of the Brontë sisters, but from what source I am unable to ascertain. After giving him credit for those abilities in his boyhood of which evidence is given in these pages, she says that: 'Popular admiration was sweet to him, and this led to his presence being sought at Arvills, and all the great village gatherings, for the Yorkshiremen have a keen relish for intellect; and it likewise procured him the undesirable distinction of having his company recommended by the landlord of the "Black Bull" to any chance traveller who might happen to feel solitary or dull over his liquor. "Do you want some one to help you with your bottle, sir? If you do, I'll send up for Patrick" (so the villagers called him to the day of his death, though, in his own family, he was always Branwell). And, while the messenger went, the landlord entertained his guest with accounts of the wonderful talents of the boy, whose precocious cleverness and great conversational powers were the pride of the village.' This account of the landlord being accustomed to send to the parsonage for Branwell to come down to the 'Bull' at Haworth on these occasions is denied by those who knew Branwell at the time, as well as by the landlord. The latter always said that he never ventured to do anything of the kind. It would have been a vulgar liberty, and an unpardonable offence to the inmates of the parsonage had he done so. Besides, the message would, in all probability, have been delivered to a servant, or perhaps to Mr. Brontë himself, or to one of his daughters, and Branwell would have been forbidden, for the credit of the family, to lend himself for such a purpose at the public-house below.

Branwell in these early days was not only the beloved of the household, but the special favourite of his aunt. This good lady was proud of her family and name, a name which her nephew bore to her infinite satisfaction, so that his sometimes rough and noisy merriment made his aunt glad, rather than grieved, because it was the true indication of health of mind and body. She easily pardoned his boyish defects: and at times, as she parted his auburn hair, she looked in his face with fondness and affection, giving him moral advice, consistent with his age, and showing him how, by sedulously cultivating the abilities with which God had blessed him, he would attain an excellent position in the world. It was this gentle and disinterested guide that Providence had placed in the stead of his mother, to impart to her son the good maxims she would herself have given him.

CHAPTER VI.

THE LITERARY TASTES OF THE CHILDREN.

The youthful Compositions of the Brontës—Character—'s Share in them—'The Secret,' a Fragment—Reading of the Brontë Children—Branwell's Character at this Period.

Mr. Brontë, perhaps, made use of a slight hyperbole when he said that, as soon as they could read and write, Charlotte and her brother and sisters used to invent and act little plays of their own; but it is certain that, at an early period of their lives, they took pleasure and pride in seeing their thoughts put down in the manifest form of written words. Charlotte, indeed, gives a list of the juvenile works she had composed. They filled twenty-two volumes, and consisted of Tales, Adventures, Lives, Meditations, Stories, Poems, Songs, &c. Without repeating all the titles which Mrs. Gaskell and others have published, it may be said that the productions manifested extraordinary ability and industry. Branwell, Emily, and Anne partook of the same spirit, and displayed similar energy according to the leisure they could command.

Before Charlotte went to Roe Head, in January, 1831, Branwell worked with his sisters in producing their monthly magazine, with its youthful stories. [12] Mrs. Gaskell has quoted Charlotte's introduction to the 'Tales of the Islanders,' one of these 'Little Magazines,' dated June, 1829, from which it appears that a remark of Branwell's led to the composition of the play of that name, and that he chose the Isle of Man as his territory, and named John Bull, Astley Cooper, and Leigh Hunt as the chief men in it. Charlotte gives the dates of most of their productions. She says: 'Our plays were established, "Young Men," June, 1826; "Our Fellows," July, 1827; "Islanders," December, 1827. These are our three great plays that are not kept secret. Emily's and my best plays were established the 1st of December, 1827; the others March, 1828. Best plays mean secret plays; they are very nice ones. All our plays are very strange ones. Their nature I need not write on paper, for I think I shall always remember them. The "Young Men's" play took its rise from some wooden soldiers Branwell had; "Our Fellows" from "Æsop's Fables;" and the "Islanders" from several events which happened.' [13]

It would be difficult to arrive at a correct understanding of the literary value of these productions of the youthful Brontës, but it would be interesting to know what kind of assistance Branwell was able to give in the work, as well as what was the general merit of these early compositions. Mrs. Gaskell makes some mention of Branwell's literary abilities in his youth. It is certain, from all we know, that his mind was as much occupied in these matters as his sisters', and that his ambition corresponded with theirs. It has, indeed, been placed on record by Mrs. Gaskell that he was associated with his sisters in the compilation of their youthful writings. This author says, also, that their youthful occupations were 'mostly of a sedentary and intellectual nature.' [14]

Among the youthful stories of which Charlotte, as has been already mentioned, wrote a catalogue or list, there was one, of which Mrs. Gaskell has published a fragment in fac-simile, written in a small, elaborate, and cramped hand—so small, indeed, as to be of little use to the general reader. In the 'Life of Charlotte Brontë,' this was inserted as a specimen of the hand-writing. It shows truly the literary ability, dramatic skill, and force of imagination of the children at the period of their lives of which I speak, and affords an interesting specimen of the character of these early works. A few extracts from it may be given here:—

THE SECRET.

CHAPTER I.

A dead silence had reigned in the Home Office of Verdopolis for three hours in the morning of a fine summer's day, interrupted only by such sounds as the scraping of a pen-knife, the dropping of a ruler, or an occasional cough; or whispered now and then some brief mandate, uttered by the noble first secretary, in his commanding tones. At length that sublime personage, after completing some score or so of despatches, addressing a small slightly-built young gentleman who occupied the chief situation among the clerks, said:

'Mr. Rymer, will you be good enough to tell me what o'clock it is?'

'Certainly, my lord!' was the prompt reply as, springing from his seat, the ready underling, instead of consulting his watch like other people, hastened to the window in order to mark the sun's situation; having made his observation, he answered: ''Tis twelve precisely, my lord.'

'Very well,' said the marquis. 'You may all give up then, and see that all your desks are locked, so that not a scrap of paper is left to litter the office. Mr. Rymer, I shall expect you to take care that my directions are fulfilled.' So saying, he assumed his hat and gloves, and with a stately tread was approaching the vestibule, when a slight bustle and whispering among the clerks arrested his steps.

'What is the matter?' asked he, turning round. 'I hope these are not sounds of contention I hear!'

'I—and—' said a broad, carrotty-locked young man of a most pugnacious aspect, 'but—but—your lordship has forgotten that—that——'

'That what?' asked the marquis, rather impatiently.

'Oh!—merely that this afternoon is a half-holiday—and—and——'

'I understand,' replied his superior, smiling, 'you need not tax your modesty with further explanation, Flanagan; the truth is, I suppose, you want your usual largess, and I'm obliged to you for reminding me—will that do?' he continued, as, opening his pocket-book, he took out a twenty-pound bank bill and laid it on the nearest desk.

'My lord, you are too generous,' Flanagan answered; but the chief secretary laughingly laid his gloved hand on his lips, and, with a condescending nod to the other clerks, sprang down the steps of the portico and strode hastily away, in order to escape the noisy expressions of gratitude which now hailed his liberality.

On the opposite side of the busy and wide street to that on which the splendid Home Office stands, rises the no less splendid Colonial Office; and, just as Arthur, Marquis of Douro, left the former structure, Edward Stanley Sydney departed from the latter: they met in the centre of the street.

'Well, Ned,' said my brother, as they shook hands, 'how are you to-day? I should think this bright sun and sky ought to enliven you if anything can.'

'Why, my dear Douro,' replied Mr. Sydney, with a faint

smile, 'such lovely, genial weather may, and I have no doubt does, elevate the spirits of the free and healthy; but for me, whose mind and body are a continual prey to all the heaviest cares of public and private life, it signifies little whether sun cheer or rain damp the atmosphere.'

'Edward,' replied Arthur, his features at the same time assuming that disagreeable expression which my landlord denominates by the term 'scorney;' 'now don't begin to bore me, Ned, with trash of that description, I'm tired of it quite: pray have you recollected that to-day is a half-holiday in all departments of the Treasury?'

'Yes; and the circumstance has cost me some money; these silly old customs ought to be abolished in my opinion— they are ruinous.'

'Why, what have you given the poor fellows?'

'Two sovereigns;' an emphatic hem formed Arthur's reply to the communication.

They had now entered Nokel Street, and were proceeding in silence past the line of magnificent shops which it contains, when the sound of wheels was heard behind them, and a smooth-rolling chariot dashed up and stopped just where they stood. One of the window-glasses now fell, a white hand was put out and beckoned them to draw near, while a silvery voice said,

'Mr. Sydney, Marquis of Douro, come hither a moment.'

Both the gentlemen obeyed the summons, Arthur with alacrity, Sydney with reluctance.

'What are your commands, fair ladies?' said the former, bowing respectfully to the inmates of the carriage, who were Lady Julia Sydney and Lady Maria Sneaky.

'Our commands are principally for your companion, my lord, not for you,' replied the daughter of Alexander the First; 'now, Mr. Sydney,' she continued, smiling on the senator, 'you must promise not to be disobedient.'

'Let me first know what I am required to perform,' was the cautious answer, accompanied by a fearful glance at the shops around.

'Nothing of much consequence, Edward,' said his wife, 'but I hope you'll not refuse to oblige me this once, love. I only want a few guineas to make out the price of a pair of earrings I have just seen in Mr. Lapis's shop.'

'Not a bit of it,' answered he. 'Not a farthing will I give you: it is scarce three weeks since you received your quarter's allowance, and if that is done already you may suffer for it.'

With this decisive reply, he instinctively thrust his hands into his breeches' pockets, and marched off with a hurried step.

'Stingy little monkey!' exclaimed Lady Julia, sinking back on the carriage-seat, while the bright flush of anger and disappointment crimsoned her fair cheek. 'This is the way he always treats me, but I'll make him suffer for it!'

'Do not discompose yourself so much, my dear,' said her companion, 'my purse is at your service, if you will accept it.'

'I am sensible of your goodness, Maria, but of course I shall not take advantage of it; no, no, I can do without the earrings—it is only a fancy, though to be sure I would rather have them.'

'My pretty cousin,' observed the marquis, who, till now, had remained a quiet though much-amused spectator of the whole scene, 'you are certainly one of the most extravagant young ladies I know: why, what on earth can you possibly want with these trinkets? To my knowledge you have at least a dozen different sorts of ear-ornaments.'

'That is true; but then these are quite of another kind; they are so pretty and unique that I could not help wishing for them.'

'Well, since your heart is so much set upon the baubles, I will see whether my purse can compass their price, if you will allow me to accompany you to Mr. Lapis's.'

'Oh! thank you, Arthur, you are very kind,' said Lady Julia, and both the ladies quickly made room for him as he sprang in and seated himself between them.

* * * * *

In a few minutes they reached the jeweller's shop. Mr. Lapis received them with an obsequious bow, and proceeded to display his glittering stores. The pendants which had so fascinated Lady Julia were in the form of two brilliant little humming-birds, whose jewelled plumage equalled if not surpassed the bright hues of nature....

This gay and pleasant fragment of a story, in which the characters and scenes are so freshly drawn, may well be imagined as one of the best, if not the best, of these productions of the Brontë children. We may, indeed, regard the spirit and style of these early stories as the outcome of their eager and observant reading of the magazine and newspaper articles within their reach—when their plastic minds would receive indelible impressions, from which they, perhaps without knowing it, acquired the knowledge and practice of accurate literary composition, and of how to clothe their thoughts in fitting words. Their retentive memories, and their intuitive faculty of putting things, brought them thus early to the threshold of the republic of letters. Mrs. Gaskell states that these works were principally written by Charlotte in a hand so small as to be 'almost impossible to decipher without the aid of a magnifying glass.' The specimen she gives is written in an upright hand, and was an attempt to represent the stories in a kind of print, as near as might be to type. If, however, Charlotte and Emily ever accustomed themselves in these early works to this diminutive type-like writing, they threw it off completely in after-years. This, Branwell never did, and Mrs. Gaskell's fac-simile page is not without some resemblance to one of his ordinary pages of manuscript reduced in size.

Mr. T. Wemyss Reid observes that Mrs. Gaskell, in speaking of the juvenile performances of the Brontë children, 'paid exclusive attention to Charlotte's productions.' 'All readers of the Brontë story,' he says, 'will remember the account of the play of "The Islanders," and other remarkable specimens, showing with what real vigour and originality Charlotte could handle her pen while she was still in the first years of her teens.' And he adds that 'those few persons who have seen the whole of the juvenile library of the family bear testimony to the fact that Branwell and Emily were at least as industrious and successful as Charlotte herself.' [15]

Even at this early period the youthful Brontës had read industriously. 'Blackwood's Magazine' had, as early as the year

1829, asserted itself to Charlotte's childish taste as 'the most able periodical there is,' and ever afterwards the whole family looked with the greatest pleasure for the brilliant essays of Christopher North and his coterie. Of other papers they saw 'John Bull' and the 'Leeds Intelligencer,' both uncompromising Conservatives, and the 'Leeds Mercury,' of the opposite party. The youthful Brontës were also readers of the 'British Essayists,' 'The Rambler,' 'The Mirror,' and 'The Lounger,' and they were great admirers of Scott.

But the advice which Charlotte afterwards gave to her friend 'E,' with regard to books for perusal, shows that their reading had been much wider: Shakespeare, Milton, Thomson, Goldsmith, Pope, Byron, Campbell, and Wordsworth; Hume, Rollin, and the 'Universal History;' Johnson's 'Poets,' Boswell's 'Johnson,' Southey's 'Nelson,' Lockhart's 'Burns,' Moore's 'Sheridan,' Moore's 'Byron,' and Wolfe's 'Remains;' and for natural history, she recommends Bewick, Audubon, White, and, strangely enough, Goldsmith. Branwell's favourite poets were Wordsworth and the melancholy Cowper, whose 'Castaway' he was always fond of quoting. The Brontës, in their young years, obtained much of their intellectual food from the circulating library at Keighley.

The extraordinary literary activity which prompted these children never afterwards left them; and Branwell, along with his sisters, was, as we have seen, the author of many effusions of remarkable character. But, as time passed on, and experience was gained, his literary productions began to acquire more vigour and polish. Yet the tone of his mind, however joyous it might be at times, recurred, when the immediate occasion had passed, to that pensive melancholy which, throughout his life, was his most marked characteristic.

Mr. Brontë looked with supreme pleasure on the growing talents of his children; but his principal hope was centred in his son, who, as he fondly trusted, should add lustre to and perpetuate his name. The boy, in these years, was precocious and lively, overflowing with humour and jollity, ready to crack a joke with the rustics he met, and all the time gathering in, with the quickest perception, impressions, both for good and ill, of human nature. Mr. Brontë sedulously, to the utmost of his power, attending to the education of Branwell, did not see the instability of his son's character, or did not apprehend any mischief from the acquaintances he had formed.

The incumbent of Haworth had distinct literary leanings, and it delighted him to find that his son had manifested literary capacity. It has been urged as somewhat of a reproach against Mr. Brontë that he did not send Branwell to a public school, but relied solely upon his own tutorship for his son's education. Situated as Mr. Brontë was, such a step as that said to have been recommended to him was unnecessary. The Grammar School adjoining was under the superintendance of a master who was well qualified to give a higher education to his pupils, if required; and Mr. Brontë himself was equally well able to do the same, but his daily duties within his chapelry left him little or no time to take upon himself the entire education of his son: all he could do was to watch and ascertain occasionally how he was progressing. Mr. Brontë, indeed, might have given the finishing touches to his son's instruction. Those, however, who knew the brilliant youth in the ripeness of his early manhood, recognized the extent of the knowledge he had acquired, and felt, too, that he had been sufficiently well-trained to know how to put it to good use.

CHAPTER VII.

YOUTH.

Charlotte goes to Roe Head—Home—at the Time—
Companion of his Sisters—Charlotte on a Visit—becomes
Interested in Pugilism—Education—Love for Music—
Retentive Memory—Personal Appearance—Spirit.

Little more of interest seems to be known concerning the
Brontës prior to the year 1831, but it is very apparent that Mr.
Brontë exercised a large influence in the formation of his children's
habits and characters. He, for instance, had a study in which he
spent a considerable portion of his time. The children had their
study also. Mr. Brontë had written poems and tales, and was wont
to tell strange stories at the breakfast-table. The children imitated
him in these things. Mr. Brontë took an enthusiastic interest in
all political matters; and here the children followed him also. In
short, they copied him in almost everything. Afterwards, he was
accustomed to hold himself up as an example for their guidance,
and to tell them how he had struggled and worked his way to the
position he held; and there is no doubt that his children had a
great admiration for his career.

Miss Branwell's influence was altogether distinct from that
of Mr. Brontë. While taking pride in the mental ability of her
nephew, she aimed at making his sisters into good housewives
and patterns of domestic and unobtrusive virtue. With this
object, turning her bed-chamber into a school-room, she taught
them to sew and to embroider; and they occupied their time in
making charity clothing, a work which she maintained 'was not

for the good of the recipients, but of the sewers; it was proper for them to do it.' Under Miss Branwell they likewise learned to clean, to wash, to bake, to cook, to make jams and jellies, with many other domestic mysteries; and here, as in everything else, they were apt pupils.

But, towards the end of the year 1830, it was decided that Charlotte should seek a wider training elsewhere; and a school, kept by Miss Wooler, at Roe Head, between Leeds and Huddersfield, was fixed upon. It was a quaint, old-fashioned house, standing in a pleasant country, which had an interest for Charlotte, for it lay not far from Hartshead, where her father's first Yorkshire curacy had been. This circumstance, together with the proximity of the remains of Kirklees priory—which had their traditions of Robin Hood—and the strange local stories she heard from Miss Wooler, led her afterwards to make this district the scene of her novel of 'Shirley.' Miss Wooler was a kind, motherly lady who took an interest in each one of her pupils. She had long been a keen observer, and knew well how to put her knowledge to use in tuition. In this school, Charlotte, a girl of sixteen, was an indefatigable student, scarcely resting in her pursuit of knowledge. She was not exactly sociable, and sat often alone with her book in play-hours—a thin fragile girl, whose brown hair overshadowed the page on which her eyes, 'those expressive orbs,' were so intently fixed. Her companions remarked at that time that she had a great store of out-of-the-way knowledge, while on some points of general information she was comparatively ignorant. But when Charlotte left Roe Head, in June, 1832, she returned to the parsonage at Haworth with more expanded ideas, and with wider knowledge, and possessing, perhaps, a keener relish for the delights of the literary world. At Roe Head Charlotte made the acquaintance of her life-long friend 'E,' and also of Mary and Martha 'T.'

The family of Brontë appears, about this time, to have been in perfect peace. Charlotte had corresponded with Branwell when she was at Roe Head, as a pupil of Miss Wooler; and Mrs. Gaskell has published portions of a letter sent from that place to him on May 17th, 1832, when he was in his fifteenth year, in which she showed her old political leanings wherein Branwell shared. It runs: 'Lately I had begun to think that I had lost all interest which I used formerly to take in politics; but the extreme pleasure I felt at the news of the Reform Bill's being thrown out by the House of Lords, and of the expulsion, or resignation, of Earl Grey, &c., convinced me that I have not as yet lost all my penchant for politics. I am extremely glad that aunt has consented to take in "Fraser's Magazine;" for though I know from your description of its general contents it will be rather uninteresting when compared with "Blackwood," still it will be better than remaining the whole year without being able to obtain a sight of any periodical whatever; and such would assuredly be the case, as, in the little wild moorland village where we reside, there would be no possibility of borrowing a work of this description from a circulating library. I hope with you that the present delightful weather may contribute to the perfect restoration of our dear papa's health; and that it may give aunt pleasant reminiscences of the salubrious climate of her native place.' [16]

Charlotte's political principles were strongly Conservative, as were those of her father, brother, and sisters, and these principles were intensified in them all by their religious opinions. They held, consistently enough, the cherished political convictions of their party, and they looked upon every concession made to liberal clamour as an inroad on the very vitals of the Constitution. Hence the jubilation of Charlotte when the Reform Bill was rejected by the House of Lords on October 7th, 1831. But the march of events, in after-years, modified their political opinions considerably.

Branwell at this period, while still under tuition at home, was the constant companion of his sisters, and frequently accompanied them on their visits to the moors and picturesque places in the neighbourhood. 'E,' writing in 'Scribner,' says: 'Charlotte's first visit from Haworth was made about three months after she left school. She travelled in a two-wheeled gig, the only conveyance to be had in Haworth except the covered-cart which brought her to school. Mr. Brontë sent Branwell as an escort; he was *then* a very dear brother, as dear to Charlotte as her own soul; they were in perfect accord of taste and feeling, and it was a mutual delight to be together. Branwell had probably never been from home before; he was in wild ecstacy with everything. He walked about in unrestrained boyish enjoyment, taking views in every direction of the turret-roofed house, the fine chestnut-trees on the lawn (one tree especially interested him because it was iron-girthed, having been split by storms, but still flourishing in great majesty), and a large rookery, which gave to the house a good background—all these he noted and commented upon with perfect enthusiasm. He told his sister he was leaving her in Paradise, and if she were not intensely happy she never would be! Happy, indeed, she then was *in himself,* for she, with her own enthusiasm, looked forward to what her brother's great promise and talent might effect. He would be, at this time, between fifteen and sixteen years of age. [17]

In the June of 1833, when Branwell was about this age, we learn that he drove his sisters with great delight in a trap, or dog-cart, to Bolton Bridge, to meet their friend 'E,' who waited for the young Brontës in a carriage at the 'Devonshire Arms.' [18] This was a visit to the ancient abbey and immemorial woods and vales of Bolton. We may well imagine from the time of the year—the 'leafy month of June,' when all nature would be glad, and the deep woods gay with varied leaves, while the Wharfe, of amber hue, foamed and rushed impetuously down its rocky channel, from the moorland hills above historic Barden, to the peaceful meads of the ruined abbey—that the hearts of the Brontës rejoiced, enchanted and impressed by these glorious and stately solitudes.

It cannot but be regretted that, while his sisters could confer in confidence and familiarity together, and enjoy a community of interests in secrecy and affection, Branwell had no brother whose sympathetic counsel he could embrace; but, thrown back upon himself, was led to seek the society of appreciative friends, who made him acquainted with the manners and customs of the world, and the vices of society, before his time had yet come to know much concerning them. It was, indeed, unfortunately, no infrequent circumstance to see the plastic, light-hearted, unsuspecting Branwell listening to the coarse jokes of the sexton of Haworth—the noted John Brown—while that functionary was employed in digging the graves so often opened in the churchyard, under the shadow of the parsonage.

It was the kind of society in which he sought relaxation at Haworth that led him to take an interest, which he long retained, in the pugilistic ring. The interest in pugilism and the 'noble art,' it must, however, be remembered, had been made fashionable by wealthy, influential, and titled people, amongst whom was Lord Byron, and by the fops and dandies of an earlier period. Jackson, the noted professor, was a great friend of the poet, and, on several occasions, visited him at Newstead. Early in this century, too, many men about town were accustomed to assemble for practice at the academy of Angelo and Jackson. Branwell, also, read with eagerness the columns of 'Bell's Life in London,' and other sporting papers of the day. The names and personal appearance of the celebrated pugilists who, at that time, to the delight of the *élite* of society, pounded each other till they were unlike anything human—for the applause of the multitude, and the honour of wearing the 'Champion's Belt,'—were familiar to him. 'Bell's Life' was taken in by an innkeeper at Haworth; and the members of the village boxing-club, one of whom was Branwell, were posted up in all public matters relating to the 'noble art of self-defence.' They had sundry boxing-gloves, and, at intervals, amused themselves with sparring in an upper room of a building at Haworth. These practices, at the time of which we speak, were but boyish amusements, and were no doubt congenial to the animal spirits and energetic temperaments of those who entered into them, and they were so more especially to Branwell, who had abundance of both. But it may be that here he became acquainted with young men whose habits and conduct had a deleterious influence upon him at the very opening of his career. If, however, Branwell's high spirit allowed him sometimes to be led away by his companions, his natural goodness of heart brought a ready and vehement repentance. The respect he felt for his father's calling, magnified, in his eyes, any fault of his own—who ought to have been more than ordinarily good—and, exaggerating his failings, he would lament his 'dreadful conduct' in deep distress. Such unmistakable evidences of sincerity and truthfulness procured him a ready pardon. He was necessarily his aunt's favourite; but he attached himself to all about him with so much readiness of affection that it is quite evident, whatever his youthful faults, they were of a superficial character only.

The studies which Branwell pursued in his youth were noticed by his literary friends, in after-years, to bear a considerable fruit of classical knowledge. He possessed then a familiar and extensive acquaintance with the Greek and Latin authors. He knew well the history and condition of Europe, and of this country, in past and present times; and his conversational powers on these, and the current literature of the day, were of the highest order. Mr. Brontë had obtained musical tuition for his son and daughters, and Branwell was enthusiastically fond of sacred music, and could play the organ. He was acquainted with the works of the great composers of recent and former times; and, although he could not perform their elaborate compositions well, he was always so excited when they were played for him by his friends that he would walk about the room with measured footsteps, his eyes raised to the ceiling, accompanying the music with his voice in an impassioned manner, and beating time with his hand on the chairs as he passed to and fro. He was an enthusiastic admirer of the oratorio of 'Samson,' which Handel deemed equal to the 'Messiah,' and of the Mass-music of Haydn, Mozart, and others. Religion had, indeed, been deeply implanted in Branwell's breast; but, whenever he heard sacred music like this, his devotional impressions were deepened, and even in times of temptation, indulgence, and folly the influence of early piety was never effaced. Among his minor accomplishments, he had acquired the practice of writing short-hand with facility, and also of writing with both hands at the same time with perfect ease, so that he possessed the extraordinary power of writing two letters at once. His hand-writing was of an upright character. Branwell, too, had a wonderful power of observation, and a most retentive memory. It is on record that, before he visited London, he so mastered its labyrinths, by a diligent study of maps and books, that he spoke with a perfect knowledge of it, and astonished inhabitants of the metropolis by his intimate acquaintance with by-ways and places of which they even had never heard. In person he was rather below the middle height, but of refined and gentleman-like appearance, and of graceful manners. His complexion was fair and his features handsome; his mouth and chin were well-shaped; his nose was prominent and of the Roman type; his eyes sparkled and danced with delight, and his fine forehead made up a face of oval form which gave an irresistible charm to its possessor, and attracted the admiration of those who knew him. Added to this, his address was simple and unadorned, yet polished; but, being familiar with the English language in its highest form of expression, and with the Yorkshire and Hibernian *patois* also, he could easily make use of the quaintest and broadest terms when occasion called for them. It was, indeed, amazing how suddenly he could pass from the discussion of a grave and lofty subject, or from a deep disquisition, or some exalted poetical theme, to one of his light-hearted and amusing Irish or Yorkshire sallies. He could be sad and joyful almost at the same time, like the sunshine and gloom of April weather; exhibiting, by anticipation, the future lights and shadows of his own sad, short, and chequered existence. In a word, he seemed at times even to be jocular and merry with gravity itself.

It is known also that Branwell, at that period of his young life—when manhood with its hopes and joys, its enterprises and aspirations, its affections and its responsibilities, stretched before him—was also busily laying, to the best of his ability, the foundations, as he trusted, of a brilliant literary or artistic future.

CHAPTER VIII.

ART-AIMS OF THE BRONTËS.

Love of Art in the Youthful Brontës—elaborate Drawings—
J. B. Leyland, Sculptor——. George Hogarth's Opinion
—Exhibition at Leeds—. William Robinson, their Drawing-
Master—aims at Portrait-Painting—. B. Leyland in
London—and the Royal Academy—visits London.

The biographers of the Brontë sisters have pointed out especially the artistic instinct of Charlotte and Emily; and the originality and fidelity of their written descriptions, and the beauty of the composition and 'colour' of their word-paintings, have formed an inexhaustible theme for the various writers on the excellencies of Brontë genius. The appreciation of art possessed by the members of this family, whether in drawing, painting, or sculpture, was manifested early; but, though highly gifted in felicity and aptness of verbal expression in describing natural scenery, and in the delineation of personal character, they were not endowed, in like degree, with the faculty of placing their ideas—weird and wild, or beautiful and joyous as they might be—in that tangible and fixed shape in which artists have perpetuated the emanations of their genius. The devotion of Charlotte and Branwell to art was, nevertheless, so intense, and their belief was so profound, at one time, that the art-faculty consisted of little more than mechanical dexterity, and could be obtained by long study and practice in manipulation, that the sister toiled incessantly in copying, almost line for line, the grand old engravings of Woollett, Brown, Fittler, and others till her eyesight was dimmed and blurred by the sedulous application; and Branwell, with the same belief, eagerly followed her example. Great talent and perseverance they undoubtedly had; and, although we are not possessed of any original drawings by Charlotte of striking character, we know that Branwell drew in pen-and-ink with much facility, humour, and originality. His productions, in this manner, will be more particularly noticed in the course of this work. Charlotte's drawings were said to be pre-Raphaelite in detail, but they had no approach to the spirit of that school; and Branwell's pictures, however meritorious they might be as likenesses of the individuals they represented, lacked, in every instance, that artistic touch which the hand of genius always gives, and cannot help giving. While at school at Roe Head, Charlotte had been noticed by her fellow-pupils to draw better and more quickly than they had before seen anyone do, and we have been told by one of them that 'she picked up every scrap of information concerning painting, sculpture, poetry, music, &c., as if it were gold.' The list she drew up a year or two earlier of the great artists whose works she wished to see, shows us that her interest in art, even in her thirteenth year, led her to read of them and their productions.

On her return home in 1832, Charlotte wrote on the 21st July respecting her course of life at the parsonage: 'In the morning, from nine o'clock till half-past twelve, I instruct my sisters, and draw; then we walk till dinner-time. After dinner I sew till tea-time, and after tea I either write, read, or do a little fancy-work, or draw as I please.' Charlotte also told Mrs. Gaskell 'that, at this period of her life, drawing, and walking with her sisters, formed the two great pleasures and relaxations of her day.'

Mr. Brontë, observing that his son and daughters took pleasure in the art of drawing, and believing this to be one of their natural gifts that ought to be cultivated, perhaps as an accomplishment which they might some time find useful in tuition, obtained for them a drawing-master. But he also observed that Branwell excelled his sisters in the art, while he likewise painted in oils, and he may at times have had some hope that his son would become a distinguished artist.

It is apparent, indeed, that drawing not only engaged much of Charlotte's leisure, but that it formed a part of home-education. Her sisters as well as herself underwent great labour in acquiring the art in these early years, and Branwell also was not behind them in industrious pursuit of the same object. Charlotte even thought of art as a profession for herself; and so strong was this intention, that she could scarcely be convinced that it was not her true vocation. In short, her appreciative spirit always dwelt with indescribable pleasure on works of real art, and she derived, from their contemplation, one of the chief enjoyments of her life. 'To paint them, in short,' says Jane Eyre, speaking of the pictures she is showing to Mr. Rochester, 'was to enjoy one of the keenest pleasures I have ever known.' [19] The love the Brontës thus cherished for art became, as time passed on, a passion, and its cultivation a pressing and sensible duty. They were not aware that their industry in, and devotion to it, as they understood it, were a misdirection of their genius. How far this love of it, and this eagerness to acquire a knowledge of the mysteries of composition and analysis, and to be possessed of art-practice and art-learning, may have been excited and encouraged by the success that had been achieved by others with whom they were familiar, in the same direction, may be surmised.

In the year of Mr. Brontë's appointment to Hartshead, there was born, at Halifax, an artist, Joseph Bentley Leyland, who was destined to become the personal friend and inspirer of Mr. Brontë's son, Branwell. Leyland, in his early boyhood, showed, by the ease and faithfulness with which he modelled in clay, or sketched with pencil, the objects that attracted his attention, the direction of his genius. The sculptor, as he grew in years, treated, with artistic power, classical subjects which had not hitherto been embodied in sculpture. At the age of twenty-one he modelled a statue of Spartacus, the Thracian, a general who, after defeating several Roman armies in succession, was overthrown with his forces by Crassus the prætor, and slain. The dead leader was represented at that moment after death before the muscles have acquired extreme rigidity. The statue, which was of colossal size, was modelled from living subjects, and was, in all respects, a production far beyond the sculptor's years. It was the most striking work of art at the Manchester Exhibition in the year 1832, and was favourably noticed in the 'Manchester Courier,' on November the 3rd of that year. Such notices were productive of increased exertion, which soon became manifest in the creation of other more lofty and successful works. Among these was a colossal bust of Satan, some six feet in height, which was pronounced to be 'truly that of Milton's "Arch-angel ruined."' Mr. George Hogarth, the father-in-law of Charles Dickens—a gentleman of literary power and knowledge—was the editor of the 'Halifax Guardian' at the time, and visited the artist's small studio, where he saw, in one corner, under its lean-to roof, for the first time, the bust of Satan. He was astonished at its merit, and published his criticism of the work in the paper on May the 24th, 1834. Leyland was then strongly urged to forward the bust to London, which he did, with some others he had modelled; and the critics were invited to visit his studio. The favourable opinion which Mr. Hogarth published, in the paper of which he was editor, was endorsed, but in more flattering terms, in the 'Morning Chronicle' of December 2nd, 1834. But there was held at Leeds, in these years, the Annual Exhibition of the Northern Society for the Encouragement of the Fine Arts; and Leyland, before he sent his work to London, included it in his contributions to the exhibition at Leeds.

The oil-paintings and water-colour drawings that were hung there, in the summer of 1834, appear to have formed a fine and varied collection. There were beautiful landscapes in water-colour by Copley Fielding, and in oil by Alexander Nasmyth, John Linnel, Robert Macreth; and others were well represented, while historical paintings by H. Fradelle, sea-pieces by Carmichael, and animal paintings by Schwanfelder, always good, were highly creditable to these well-known names. A number of fine portraits by William Bewick and William Robinson added interest and beauty to the galleries. The reader may conceive, if he will, the Brontës—Charlotte and Branwell, and, it may be, Mr. Brontë and Emily—enjoying to the full the paintings and sculptures which were before them. He may fancy the suddenly expressed, 'Look, Charlotte!' as some newly discovered picture flashed as a keen delight on the eager fancy of Branwell's appreciative spirit. He may imagine the ready criticism of Charlotte, and the attempts which she and her brother made to divine how much thought had gone to make up the composition of a work. The young Brontë critics, as they looked on the colossal head of Satan—on the stern and inflexible firmness of the features 'whose superhuman beauty is yet covered with a cloud of the deepest melancholy;' on the representation 'of the great and glorious being sunk in utter despair,'—might ponder, perhaps, whether an ideal has dawned upon the imagination of the artist, and so been wrought from no model, but from the vision of his meditations, or whether success is, after all, but the evidence of painful elaboration. At any rate, it was just on such an exhibition of paintings and works of art that Charlotte and Branwell delighted to dwell in intelligent and educated observation.

That a new impetus and a new meaning were given to their art-practice about this time is certain, and it was probably not long after this date that Mr. Brontë engaged, for the instruction of his son and daughters, an artist of Leeds, the Mr. William Robinson I have mentioned as having contributed a number of portraits to the exhibition. The object of the Brontës was now to practise painting, and this able instructor was consequently engaged.

Mr. Robinson was a native of Leeds, who had, by natural talent and steady perseverance, acquired something more than a local reputation. His early love of art had been such that the wishes of his friends failed to divert him from its pursuit, and he received lessons from Mr. Rhodes, sen., of Leeds, an admirable painter in water-colours. But Mr. Robinson had a strong predilection for portrait-painting, to which he had devoted his powers, at the same time availing himself of every opportunity for improving in its practice. In the year 1820, he visited the metropolis, taking with him an introduction to Sir Thomas Lawrence, who received him with great kindness, and he became a pupil of this eminent artist. Sir Thomas, however, with noble generosity, declined any remuneration whatever, and Robinson assisted his master in his work. He was introduced to Fuseli, and gained the privilege of studying at the Royal Academy, his work being characterized by the requisite merit. He was stimulated to renewed exertion by this much desired success. In 1824, he had returned to his native town, where he procured numerous commissions. He was subsequently introduced to Earl de Grey, of whom he painted portraits, as also of his family. Mr. Robinson, in addition, painted four portraits for the United Service Club, one of which was of the Duke of Wellington, who honoured him with several sittings. Besides these, amongst his other works, was a portrait of the Princess Sophia, and a copy of one of the Duke of York for the Duchess of Gloucester. It was from this gentleman that Branwell Brontë and his sister received a few lessons in portrait-painting at the time of which I speak, and a knowledge of the master's career did not a little to fire the mind of the enthusiastic Branwell with ardour to aim in the same direction, while the contemporary efforts of others added fuel to the fire.

At this time there were certain artists of the neighbourhood who were trying their fortunes in London, and who were known to Branwell Brontë by reputation: C. H. Schwanfelder, the animal painter, and John W. Rhodes, the son of the artist under whom Mr. Robinson had studied. The father of the latter had endeavoured to dissuade him from making art his profession, but all to no purpose: the bent of his genius could not be curbed. He painted in water-colour and oil with great beauty and fidelity; the green lane, the wild flower hanging from an old wall, were his subjects. His works met with well-deserved encomiums in the London press, and with praise wherever they were exhibited; but, when full of aspiring hopes, he was attacked, like Girtin, Liversedge, and Bonnington, by inflammation in the eyes, and ill health. He died at the early age of thirty-three, and a memoir of him appeared in 'The Art Journal' of March, 1843. The determination of Charlotte and Branwell to take, as it were, the Temple of Art by forcible possession, was, it may be conceived, due also, in some measure, to the growing celebrity of Leyland; for, in literature and art, Halifax was nearer to the Brontës than any of the surrounding towns. The praise of Leyland's works, moreover, had been re-published from the London press in all the papers of his native county, and poetic eulogies appeared in the 'Leeds Intelligencer' and in the 'Leeds Mercury;' and, therefore, that they were eager to emulate his works and to equal his success seems very probable.

I have felt it necessary to mention these influences, as they alone serve to explain how it was that Branwell and his sister were led to think of, and—as regards the brother—to persist for a time in making a profession of painting for which they had no special aptitude. Branwell, in fact, designed to become himself a portrait-painter, and he conceived that a course of instruction at the Royal Academy afforded the best means of preparation for that profession.

Being gifted with a keen and distinct observation, combined with the faculty of retaining impressions once formed, and being an excellent draughtsman, he could with ease produce admirable representations of the persons he portrayed on canvas. But it is quite clear that he never had been instructed either in the right mode of mixing his pigments, or how to use them when properly prepared, or, perhaps, he had not been an apt scholar. He was, therefore, unable to obtain the necessary flesh tints, which require so much delicacy in handling, or the gradations of light and shade so requisite in the painting of a good portrait or picture. Had Branwell possessed this knowledge, the portraits he painted would have been valuable works from his hand; but the colours he used have all but vanished, and scarcely any tint, beyond that of the boiled oil with which they appear to have been mixed, remains. Yet, even if Branwell had been fortunate in his work, he would only have attained the position, probably, of a moderate portrait-painter. His ambition, however, took a higher range, and he prepared himself for the venture, hoping that the desiderata which Haworth could not supply would be amply provided for him in London, when the long-desired opportunity arrived.

At Haworth he had been industrious, for he had painted some portraits of the members of his family, and of several friends. One of these is well described by Mrs. Gaskell, and her account is worth giving here:—'It was a group of his sisters, life-size, three-quarters length ... the likenesses were, I should think, admirable. I only judge of the fidelity with which the other two were depicted, from the striking resemblance which Charlotte, upholding the great frame of canvas, and consequently standing right behind it, bore to her own representation, though it must have been ten years and more since the portraits were taken. The picture was divided, almost in the middle, by a great pillar. On the side of the column which was lighted by the sun stood Charlotte, in the womanly dress of that day of gigot sleeves and large collars. On the deeply shadowed side was Emily, with Anne's gentle face resting on her shoulder. Emily's countenance struck me as full of power; Charlotte's of solicitude; Anne's of tenderness. The two younger seemed hardly to have attained their full growth, though Emily was taller than Charlotte; they had cropped hair and a more girlish dress. I remember looking on these two sad, earnest, shadowed faces, and wondering whether I could trace the mysterious expression which is said to foretell an early death. I had some fond superstitious hope that the column divided their fate from hers who stood apart in the canvas, as in life she survived. I liked to see that the bright side of the pillar was towards *her*—that the light in the picture fell on *her*. I might more truly have sought in her presentment—nay, in her living

84

face—for the sign of death in her prime.' [20]

From Mrs. Gaskell's description of this one picture, it is apparent that Branwell possessed, not only the faculty, as we have seen, of obtaining excellent portraits, but that he had the ability to impress the faces of his sisters with thought, intelligence, and sensibility; and to invest them with the habitual expressions they wore, of power, solicitude, and tenderness. The deep reflection which Branwell bestowed on this picture, and the care he lavished on its mysterious composition, show unquestionably the aptitude and capacity of his own mind, which enabled him to obtain these essential expressions; and it is evident that his peculiarity of thought invested his picture with that sadness and gloom which, in after times, tinctured the poems he wrote under the solemn-sounding pseudonym of 'Northangerland.' This picture is only one among many others he painted in preparing himself for his intended studies at the Royal Academy; and the old nurse, Nancy Garrs, tells me that he often wanted to paint her portrait, but she told him that she did not think herself 'good-looking enough.'

At a later date Branwell related to Mr. George Searle Phillips the story of his artistic hopes. [21] He spoke of the great fondness for drawing manifested by the whole family; and declared that Charlotte, especially, was well read in art-learning, and knew the lives of the old masters, whose works she criticized with discrimination and judgment. But he said that she had ruined her eyesight by making minute copies of line-engravings, on one of which she was occupied six months. He also spoke of his own passionate love of art, and of the bright and confident anticipations with which he had looked forward to his projected studies at the Royal Academy, which had been the cherished hope of his family and himself.

Leyland had visited London in the December of 1833, when he obtained from Stothard a letter of introduction to Ottley, the curator of the Elgin Marbles, to allow him to study the marbles in the British Museum. Permission was readily granted, and the sculptor availed himself of it. A year later Leyland took up his residence in the metropolis. He was received in a friendly manner by Chantrey and Westmacott, the latter inviting him to dinner, and afterwards showing him his foundry at Pimlico, and his works in progress, among which was the statue of the Duke of York. He was also introduced to, and enjoyed the friendship of Nasmyth—the father of the eminent engineer whose story has recently been given to the world—and of Warley: one a landscape-painter of celebrity, and the other famed as an artist in water-colour. The latter, who had considerable faith in astrology, persisted in drawing the younger sculptor's horoscope. Among others, he became known to Haydon, under whom he subsequently studied anatomy. This lamented artist was a genuine friend, and it was under his instructions that Leyland perfected his natural perception of the grand and beautiful in art. While here he modelled, in life-size, a figure of 'Kilmeny,' in illustration of the passage in Hogg's 'Queen's Wake,' where the sinless maiden is awakened by Elfin music in fairy-land. It was a successful work, and was favourably noticed by the critics. It was subsequently purchased for the Literary and Philosophical Society of his native town.

It was while Leyland was in the metropolis that Charlotte wrote, on the 6th July, 1835:

'We are all about to divide, break up, separate. Emily is going to school, Branwell is going to London, and I am going to be a governess. This last determination I formed myself, knowing that I should have to take the step sometime, "and better sune as syne," to use the Scotch proverb; and knowing well that papa would have enough to do with his limited income, should Branwell be placed at the Royal Academy, and Emily at Roe Head.'

While this project was warmly engaging the attention of the Brontë family, Leyland was living in London, at the house of Mr. Geller, a mezzotinto-engraver, who was a native of Bradford; and, at the time, the sculptor modelled a group of three figures illustrative of a passage in Maturin's tragedy of 'Bertram,' which represented the warrior listening to the prior reading. The work was engraved by Geller. This group was said to be conceived in the 'true spirit of Maturin,' and met with the favourable notice of the London periodicals of the year 1835, the year of Branwell's visit to the metropolis. The reviews were also reproduced in most of the Yorkshire papers.

The design of putting Branwell forward as an artist, and of giving him the opportunity and the means of beginning and continuing his studies, where he might be imbued with the spirit of the great sculptors and painters who have left imperishable names, and whose works are stored in the public art-galleries of London, had at last been determined upon. The sacrifices the Brontë family were prepared to make in order to secure this object require but a passing notice here. Branwell was a treasured brother; and they would feel, no doubt, a sincere happiness in promoting his interests, in furthering his views, and in bringing his artistic abilities before the world. It would, however, seem scarcely possible that the difficulties attending Branwell's admission as a student at the Royal Academy had been duly considered. He could not be admitted without a preliminary examination of his drawings from the antique and the skeleton, to ascertain if his ability as a draughtsman was of such an order as would qualify him for studentship; and, if successful in this, he would be required to undergo a regular course of education, and to pass through the various schools where professors and academicians attended to give instruction. No doubt it was wished that Branwell should have a regular and prolonged preparation for his professional artistic career; but it would have lasted for years, and the pecuniary strain consequent upon it would, perhaps, have been severely felt, even if Branwell's genius had justified the outlay. But there is no evidence that he ever subjected himself to the preliminary test, or made an application even to be admitted as a probationer.

It would seem that, so far as Mr. Brontë was concerned, his promotion of the wishes of his children arose rather from a desire to gratify them. It does not appear that he had any over-sanguine expectation that Branwell could carry out his ardent intention of becoming an artist. Mr. Brontë's own wish was, indeed, that his son should adopt his profession, but the mercurial youth was probably little attracted by the functions of the clergyman's office.

To London Branwell, however, went, where, without doubt, his object was to draw from the Elgin Marbles, and to study the pictures at the Royal Academy and other galleries, with a perfectly honest intention. Whatever impression he may have received of his own powers as an artist, when he saw those of the great painters of the time, we have no certain knowledge; but it does not exceed belief that he was discouraged when he looked upon the brilliant chef d'oeuvres of Sir Joshua Reynolds, Gainsborough, Sir Thomas Lawrence, and others; and that, when he reflected on the immeasurable distance between his own works and theirs, his hopes of a brilliant artistic career were partially dissipated. Whether it was due to these circumstances, or that he had become more fully aware of the early struggles that meet all who attempt art as a profession, or that his courage failed him at the contemplation of the unhappy lot which falls to those who, either from lack of talent or through misfortune, fail to make their mark in the artistic world; or whether it was because his father was unable to support him in London during the years of preparation and study for the professional career,—the requirements of which had not been sufficiently considered,—is not now accurately known. Branwell, during his short stay in London, visited most of the public institutions; and, among other places, Westminster Abbey, the western façade of which he some time afterwards sketched from memory with an accuracy that astonished his acquaintance, Mr. Grundy.

Before he left the metropolis, Branwell could not resist a visit to the Castle Tavern, Holborn, then kept by the veteran prize-fighter, Tom Spring, a place frequented by the principal sporting characters of the time. A gentleman named Woolven, who was present through the same curiosity which led Branwell there, noticed the young man, whose unusual flow of language and strength of memory had so attracted the attention of the spectators that they had made him umpire in some dispute arising about the dates of certain celebrated battles. Branwell and he became personal friends in after-years.

Branwell returned to the parsonage a wiser man. His disappointment that he was not to do as others were doing, whom he wished to emulate, was very great, but he was not yet finally discouraged. We shall see subsequently to what purpose Branwell put his artistic knowledge. The failure of the hopes regarding his academical career in art was keenly felt by his family. It was grievous as it was humiliating, but it was borne with exemplary patience and resignation. When these painful experiences had impressed the Brontë sisters with the hopelessness of high artistic study for Branwell, and when their eyes were opened to the consciousness that their large gifts did not include art, Charlotte wrote, in her novel of 'Villette,' under the character of Lucy Snowe: 'I sat bent over my desk, drawing—that is, copying an elaborate line-engraving, tediously working up my copy to the finish of the original, for that was my practical notion of art; and, strange to say, I took extreme pleasure in the labour, and could even produce curiously finished fac-similes of steel or mezzotinto plates—things about as valuable as so many achievements in worsted work, but I thought pretty well of them in those days.'

CHAPTER IX.

CHARLOTTE AT ROE HEAD.

Charlotte returns as a Teacher, with Emily as a Pupil, to Roe
Head—Determination to Maintain themselves—'s Fears
respecting Emily—'s religious Melancholy—Accuses herself
of Flippancy—is on the Borders of Despair—to Know
More of the World—at Law Hill, Halifax, as a Teacher—'s
Excitability—She returns Home out of Health.

'We are all about to divide, break up, separate,' Charlotte said,
when conveying to her friend the news of the Academy project,
and of her determination to enter upon life as a governess. If
Branwell's ambition had encouraged her own, its failure made
no change in her plans. She was 'sad,' she says, 'very sad,' at the
thoughts of leaving home; yet she was going back to the school of
Miss Wooler, whom she both loved and respected, to live at Roe
Head, this time to teach, it is true, instead of to be taught. But
her sister Emily was to accompany her, as a pupil of the school,
and that they would be together was a consolation to both sisters;
and Charlotte, too, would be near the homes of the friends she
had made when she was herself a pupil there. It was a pleasure to
think she would be able to see them sometimes.

At the end of July, then, the two proceeded to Roe Head. This
was the first of those adventurous moves which the sisters, from
time to time, made. One of the strongest features, indeed, in
their lives is the persistency with which they essayed to maintain
themselves, even when no apparently pressing necessity impelled
them. Yet we may not doubt that one sad reflection sometimes

moved them, and it was that their father's stipend ceased with his life; that they had no other resource beyond their own endeavours; and that, such was the uncertainty of all human concerns, they might at any moment be deprived of home, support, and shelter. It behoved them then to secure by their personal energies, while they were able, the very means of subsistence.

When Mr. Brontë saw his young family around him, and when he enjoyed the comfort of his hearth, the contingency of his death, and the consequent helplessness of his children, often struck him with apprehension and sadness. But he had the alleviation that they inherited, in a marked degree, his own adventurous and energetic disposition, whose successful career was always before them as an example and incentive to honourable endeavour.

Mr. Brontë looked back with just satisfaction on the early sacrifices he had made to advance himself in the world. His children were familiar with the story of his exertions. They, however, with far higher talents, were not possessed of the physical strength and powers of endurance which had aided his progress; and Charlotte and Emily, when any unusual strain was cast upon them, soon felt their strength exhausted, and they suffered depression of spirits as the consequence. Home-sickness was the great trouble of the younger sister, and, before she had been long at school, Emily grew pale and ill. Charlotte felt in her heart that, if she remained, she would die; and, at the end of three months, she returned to Haworth, where, alone among the moors, with all the wild things of nature, which had inspired so deep an interest in her feelings, she could be contented. But the youngest sister, Anne, came to Roe Head in her place, and she and Charlotte seem to have been very happy there for some time; but a tendency to religious melancholy had been developing in the elder sister's mind, imperceptibly, out of her deep religious feeling, and it increased upon her.

So early as the letter to 'E,' July 6th, 1835, she had spoken of 'duty, necessity, these are stern mistresses,' as controlling her action in seeking a situation. Her friend Mary went to see her, and in her letter to Mrs. Gaskell she says: 'I asked her how she could give so much for so little money, when she could live without it. She owned that, after clothing herself and Anne, there was nothing left, though she had hoped to be able to save something. She confessed it was not brilliant, but what could she do? I had nothing to answer. She seemed to have no interest or pleasure beyond the feeling of duty, and, when she could get, used to sit alone and "make out." She told me afterwards, that one evening she had sat in the dressing-room until it was quite dark, and then, observing it all at once, had taken sudden fright.' Some relaxation was gained by the Midsummer holidays of the year 1836. All the family were at home, and their friend 'E' visited them, so that a pleasant period of mental diversion was secured. But, after her return to her school, despondency came upon her again, and crowded her thoughts; and she wrote respecting her feelings in religious concerns: 'I do wish to be better than I am. I pray fervently sometimes to be made so. I have stings of conscience, visitings of remorse, glimpses of holy, of inexpressible things, which formerly I used to be a stranger to; it may all die away, and I may be in utter midnight, but I implore a merciful Redeemer, that, if this be the dawn of the Gospel, it may still brighten to perfect day. Do not mistake me—do not think I am good; I only wish to be so. I only hate my former flippancy and forwardness. Oh! I am no better than ever I was. I am in that state of horrid, gloomy uncertainty that, at this moment, I would submit to be old, grey-haired, to have passed all my youthful days of enjoyment, and to be settling on the verge of the grave, if I could only thereby insure the prospect of reconciliation to God, and a redemption through His Son's merits. I never was exactly careless of these matters, but I have always taken a clouded and repulsive view of them; and now, if possible, the clouds are gathering darker, and a more oppressive despondency weighs on my spirits. You have cheered me, my darling; for one moment, for an atom of time, I thought I might call you my own sister in the spirit; but the excitement is past, and I am now as wretched and hopeless as ever.'

Let us not under-estimate the mental suffering which could dictate this confession. Happily, this was not constantly present, nor her feelings always so acutely wrought upon. Even in the same letter from which the above is taken, she wishes her friends should know the thrill of delight which she experienced when she saw the packet of her friend thrown over the wall by the bearer, passing in his gig to Huddersfield Market. She persevered in her place, the whole tendency of her exaggerated reasoning forbidding her to seek that ease and relaxation which she needed so much; but she was not incapacitated for her duties, and probably her family were quite unaware of her troubles: so she remained.

Branwell and Emily were resolved not to be behind their sister in their endeavours, and they were full of anxiety to know more of the world than they could meet with at Haworth. Emily obtained a similar situation to Charlotte's, in a large school at Law Hill, near Halifax, where she found her duties far from light. Her extreme reserve with strangers is remembered by one who knew her there, but she was not at all of an unkindly nature; on the contrary, her disposition was generous and considerate to those with whom she was on familiar terms: her stay at Law Hill terminated at the end of six months. The place of her sojourn is a lofty elevation, overlooking Halifax. Emily would find the situation of the school agreeable to her taste, and to her delight in the weird and grand as presented by the solemn heath-grown heights of the West-Riding: besides, the air was as pure as that of Haworth, and Law Hill commanded finer views, among which the range of Oxenhope moors, in her father's chapelry, was visible. In the other direction, she could overlook the more cultivated district of Hartshead and Kirklees, and could see Roe Head, where her sisters Charlotte and Anne resided. Branwell also, emulating his sisters, obtained the situation of usher in the locality, which he retained for a few months.

Some adventures with their literary productions interested

them at the close of this year, of which I shall have further to speak. Miss Wooler's removal of her school to Dewsbury Moor was, in some respects, unfortunate for the sisters, as the situation was less healthy than the former one, and, when Charlotte and Anne returned home at Christmas, in the year 1837, neither was well. Charlotte's nerves were over-strung, and Anne was suffering from chest affections, which conjured up anew their recollection of the deaths of Maria and Elizabeth from consumption. To add to their troubles, Tabby fell on the ice in the lane, and fractured her leg. The consequence of this was, that they had to forego the expected pleasure of a visit from their friend 'E,' through their attendance on the old servant, whom they were unwilling should be removed to her friends, however desirable this might be on many grounds. They even went so far as to refuse to eat at all, till their aunt, who had arranged the matter to the satisfaction of all concerned, except her nieces, should give up her intention of removing Tabby. They succeeded, and Tabby remained at the parsonage, where in time she became convalescent, and Charlotte was enabled to visit her friends before she resumed her occupation.

Charlotte again returned to her accustomed duties, her nervousness increasing, not the less; and Mrs. Gaskell says: 'About this time she would turn sick and trembling at any sudden noise, and could hardly repress her screams when startled.' Through Miss Wooler's urgency, she was induced to consult a medical man, who advised her immediate return to Haworth, where quiet and rest had become for her imperatively necessary. Then her father sought for her the companionship of her two friends, Mary and Martha T——, than whose society Charlotte had never known a more rousing pleasure. They came to stay at the parsonage, and their cheerful converse and agreeable manners greatly improved Charlotte's health and spirits. We obtain an interesting picture of the young party in the following letter that Charlotte addressed to her friend 'E,' which Mrs. Gaskell has published:

'HAWORTH,

'JUNE 9TH, 1838.

'I received your packet of despatches on Wednesday; it was brought me by Mary and Martha, who have been staying at Haworth for a few days; they leave us to-day. You will be surprised at the date of this letter. I ought to be at Dewsbury Moor, you know; but I stayed as long as I was able, and at length I neither could nor dared stay any longer. My health and spirits had utterly failed me, and the medical man whom I consulted enjoined me, as I valued my life, to go home. So home I went, and the change has at once roused and soothed me. I am now, I trust, fairly in the way to be myself again.

'A calm and even mind like yours cannot conceive the feelings of the shattered wretch who is now writing to you, when, after weeks of mental and bodily anguish not to be described, something like peace began to dawn again. Mary is far from well. She breathes short, has a pain in her chest, and frequent flushings of fever. I cannot tell you what agony these symptoms give me; they remind me so strongly of my two sisters, whom no power of medicine could save. Martha is now very well; she has kept in a continual flow of good humour during her stay here, and has consequently been very fascinating....

'They are making such a noise about me, I cannot write any more. Mary is playing on the piano; Martha is chattering as fast as her little tongue can run; and Branwell is standing before her, laughing at her vivacity.'

Branwell, in these days, was well enough, and could be lively enough, when occasion served. He had his hopes, his enthusiasm yet: but, in after-years, he was to fall into a yet deeper and more serious depression than that through which Charlotte had passed.

CHAPTER X.

BRANWELL BRONTË AND HIS SISTERS' BIOGRAPHERS.

The Light in which Biographers have regarded
Branwell——. Gaskell—Causes which led her into Error—
of Branwell's Friends—. George Searle Phillips—Branwell as
Depicted by Mr. T. Wemyss Reid—. F. H. Grundy's Notice
of Branwell—A. Mary F. Robinson's Portrait of Branwell.

It will be well here—before we reach the periods of Branwell's
life that have been misunderstood—to pause, in our sketch of
the Brontë family, in order to consider certain circumstances
regarding him, which it will be impossible for any future writer
on the Brontës to disregard. It is especially necessary to consider
them in a book which—while dealing with the Brontë sisters,
their lives and their works—proposes, as a special aim, to make
Branwell's position clear. When Derwent Coleridge wrote the
short biography of his father, which is prefixed to the poet's
works, he approached the subject in a somewhat regretful way,
asking if the public has a right to inquire as to that part of a
poet's life which does not influence his fellow-men after death,
and declaring that the privacy of the dead is sacred. He felt too
keenly that the sanctity of Coleridge's life had been broken in
upon by those who lacked both accurate knowledge and just
discretion. It is a source of sincere regret to the writer of this
volume that he, too, is compelled by circumstances to treat a
part of his work almost in a deprecatory spirit, and sometimes to
assume the position of defence. For, if the failings of Coleridge
have been discovered and fed upon by those whose curiosity

leads them to delight in such things, what shall we say of Patrick Branwell Brontë, whose misdeeds have not only been sought out with a persistency worthy of a better cause, but have also been exaggerated and misrepresented to a great degree, and whose whole life, moreover, has been contorted by writers who have endeavoured to find in it some evidence for their own hypotheses? It has been the misfortune of Branwell that his life has, to some extent, been already several times written by those who have had some other object in view, and who, consequently, have not been studious to acquire a correct view of the circumstances of it. These writers, it will be seen, have therefore, perhaps unavoidably, fallen into many grievous errors regarding him, so that his name, at this day, has come to be held up as a reproach and even as a token of ignominy. If it be remembered that Mrs. Gaskell, in her 'Life of Charlotte Brontë,' describes him as a drunkard and an opium-eater, as one who rendered miserable the lives of his sisters, and might very well have shot his father; that Mr. T. Wemyss Reid, in his 'Charlotte Brontë, a Monograph,' has spoken of him as 'this lost and degraded man;' that Miss Robinson, in her 'Emily Brontë,' has called him a 'poor, half-demented lonely creature,' and has moralized upon his 'vulgar weakness,' his 'corrupt and loathsome sentimentality,' and his 'maudlin Micawber penitence;' and lastly that Mr. Swinburne, in a notice of the last-named work in the 'Athenæum,' has said, 'of that lamentable and contemptible caitiff—contemptible not so much for his common-place debauchery as for his abject selfishness, his lying pretension, and his nerveless cowardice—there is far too much in this memoir;' it may well appear that we have here a strange subject for a biography.

But, since the publication of Miss Robinson's 'Emily Brontë,'—in which Branwell is specially degraded,—it has been felt by many admirers of the Brontës that it was desirable his life should be treated independently of the theories and necessities of his sisters' biographers, and in a spirit not unfriendly to him; for there are many people who believe that Branwell's genius has never been sufficiently recognized, and there are a few who know that, notwithstanding his many failings and misdeeds, the charges made against him are, not a few of them, wholly untrue, while many more are grossly exaggerated, and that his disposition and character have been wholly misrepresented. Having in my possession many of his letters and poems, and having been personally acquainted with him, I have undertaken the task of telling the story of his life in connection with the lives of his sisters, for I think that there is much in his strange and sad history that ought to be known, while sufficient evidence exists of his mental power to prove that he was a worthy member of the intellectual family to which he belonged. It may not be amiss here, in order to illustrate circumstances that will be alluded to in parts of this work, to touch slightly upon the bibliography of Branwell's life, and endeavour to discover the causes which have contributed to the ill-repute in which he is generally held.

Mrs. Gaskell, who became acquainted with Charlotte Brontë after the deaths of her brother and sisters, when all that was most sorrowful in her life had been enacted, saw, or thought she saw, in her the evidences of a deep dejection, the result of a life passed under circumstances of misery and depression. In her 'Life of Charlotte Brontë,' this writer's endeavour to trace the successive influences of the trials of Charlotte's life upon her, and to find in them the explanation of what was, perhaps, in some measure, an idiosyncrasy of character, has led her, in the strength of her own preconception, to interpret many circumstances to the attestation of her theory. Such, at all events, is the explanation which Mr. T. Wemyss Reid has offered, in his 'Charlotte Brontë, a Monograph,' of the partial manner in which Mrs. Gaskell has dealt with certain of Miss Brontë's letters. If we conceive Mrs. Gaskell writing with this preconception, tending to give undue weight to all that was unhappy in the history of her heroine, we need feel little surprise that her account of the lives of the Brontës is too often a gloomy one, that their isolation at Haworth, their poverty, and their struggles have been exaggerated, or that, in order to throw in a sombre background to her picture, she was unduly credulous in listening to those unfounded stories with which she made Mr. Brontë to appear, in act, at least, diabolical, and which have helped to depict the career of Patrick Branwell Brontë in such dark and tragic colours. She had heard at Haworth the story of his disgrace, his subsequent intemperance, and his death. Herein she believed was the great sorrow of the sisters' minds, the care which had induced a morbid peculiarity in their writings, and cast a shadow upon their lives. Mrs. Gaskell seems to have thought it devolved upon her, not merely to picture beginnings of evil in the brother, and trace them to his ruin; but, also, to punish the lady whom she held responsible for what has been termed 'Branwell's fall.' To this end she thought it right to lay at the lady's door, in part, the premature deaths of the sisters; and, in sustaining the idea that the effect on them of the brother's disgrace was what she believed it to be, she was led to employ partial versions of the letters, and exaggerate the whole course of Branwell's conduct. Her book was read with astonishment by those whose characters were made to suffer by it, and she was obliged, in later editions, to omit the charges against the lady; and also those against Mr. Brontë. But Mrs. Gaskell still maintained that, whatever the cause, the effect was the same.

It was not believed at the time, by some, that, because Mrs. Gaskell had been obliged to withdraw the statements complained of, in the later editions of her work, they were necessarily untrue. Mr. Thackeray had said that the life was 'necessarily incomplete, though most touching and admirable,' and the original edition was still in circulation, and was pirated abroad.

The friends of Branwell Brontë, those who from actual acquaintance knew his mental power and real disposition, resented greatly the wrong that had been done to his memory; and several representations were made in his favour. One of these was in an article entitled: 'A Winter's Day at Haworth,' published in 'Chambers's Journal,' 1869. Mr. George Searle Phillips, in the 'Mirror,' of 1872, also published some valuable reminiscences which tended to show Branwell's true elevation of character and gentleness of disposition.

The publication of Mr. Wemyss Reid's 'Charlotte Brontë, a Monograph,' in the year 1877, while it called attention to the original view of Branwell's life and character, did not aim to remove it. Mr. Reid repudiated, with success, the idea that the effect of Branwell's career upon Charlotte and Emily was what Mrs. Gaskell represented it to have been, without expressing any dissent from the story itself. This writer does not, indeed, appear to have suspected that the explanation was to be found in the fact that Branwell was not so bad as he had been made to appear, or that Mrs. Gaskell had fallen into other errors besides those of the letters which he corrected. But, though Mr. Reid carefully avoided the reproduction of the details of Mrs. Gaskell's account of Branwell's life, what reference is made to him in the 'Monograph,' after the period of his youth, is always in terms of reprobation, which have done nothing to discourage belief in the suppressed scandal. Moreover, Mr. Reid revived some of the charges against Mr. Brontë, and painted a sinister portrait of him.

It was under these circumstances that Mr. F. H. Grundy, C.E., another friend of Branwell's, in his 'Pictures of the Past' (1879), endeavoured to do some justice to his memory, and declared, notwithstanding his great failings, that his abilities were of a very high order, and his disposition one that should be admired. I have found Mr. Grundy's materials of use in this work. But, unfortunately, this friend of Branwell's wrote from recollection, and made such great mistakes in the chronology of his life that his account did not give a true interpretation of actual circumstances. Mr. Grundy, too, had evidently refreshed his memory with a perusal of Mrs. Gaskell's volume, and so his information was considerably tinctured with that writer's misconceptions. This notice had the very opposite effect to that which was intended, and has since been largely used by writers whose purpose has led them to rank Branwell with the fallen.

In Miss Robinson's recently published 'Emily Brontë,' the scandal of Branwell's life, which Mrs. Gaskell laid before the reading world, has been reproduced, and her evil report of his character greatly increased. 'Why,' it might well be asked, 'should it be necessary to publish the records of a brother's misdeeds as a conspicuous feature in a sister's memoir? Why revive a scandal that has been so long suppressed?' Miss Robinson has, indeed, given her reason, in that Branwell's sins had so large a share in determining the bent of his sister's genius, that 'to have passed them by would have been to ignore the shock which turned the fantasy of the "poems" into the tragedy of "Wuthering Heights,"' and here, probably, is the only adequate purpose that could have been found in doing so; but it is scarcely sufficient to explain why Miss Robinson has, almost from her first mention of Branwell Brontë to her remarks on his death, treated every act of his life with contumely, censure, and contempt, or that she has, in opposition to every previous opinion, represented his abilities as almost void. While Mr. Reid suggested that Emily Brontë, in writing her novel, must have obtained some of her impressions from her brother's conduct, Mr. Grundy had made a statement tending to show that Branwell had written a portion of the story himself. If Branwell's abilities were no better than Miss Robinson says they were, she has disposed of Mr. Grundy's assertion at once; but not the less does she employ other reasons for that end, and the degradation she has thought it necessary to show in Branwell, answers quite as much to prove the impossibility of his having written the work, as to picture the cause of brooding in Emily, under which she produced the tragedy of 'Wuthering Heights.'

With views similar to those with which Mrs. Gaskell wrote, Miss Robinson, in following the biographer of Charlotte, has fallen into the same errors. In order to make it clear that the part Branwell had in the production of 'Wuthering Heights,' by his sister, was subjective, this writer has found it necessary to show in his life much of what is worst in the characters of the story. So completely has Miss Robinson carried out this portion of her work, that Mr. Swinburne was led to say, in his notice of it, that 'Emily Brontë's tenderness for the lower animals ... was so vast as to include even her own miserable brother.' [22] But Miss Robinson has not succeeded so far without much unfairness to the victim of her theory, in omissions and errors of fact. I shall have occasion to treat at some length, later, Branwell's relationship both to 'Wuthering Heights' and 'The Tenant of Wildfell Hall.'

I hope, indeed, to be able to prove that Branwell was (as all who personally knew him aver him to have been) a man of great and powerful intellectual gifts, to relieve his memory of much of the obloquy that has been heaped upon it, and to clearly show the remarkable individuality of his character. I shall find it necessary, in doing so, to take exception to the portions of Mrs. Gaskell's 'Life of Charlotte Brontë' which deal with her brother, as to some extent I had to do to those which refer to Mr. Brontë. More especially, however, will it be necessary to deal with the fuller statements in the first edition of the work, and with their repetition and amplification in the more recent volumes of Mr. Reid and Miss Robinson.

I have thought it necessary to introduce these remarks in this place, in order that the reader, when he comes to the consideration of certain statements made by previous writers concerning Branwell, and his relationship with his sisters, may have a clear understanding of the views with which the works containing these statements have been written.

CHAPTER XI.

———————————

BRANWELL AT BRADFORD.

Branwell becomes a Freemason—His love of Art
undiminished—Instruction in Oil-Painting—Portrait-
Painting at Bradford—Commissions—Letter to
Mr. Thompson, the Artist —Robinson's Charges of
Misconduct—Erroneous Statements —'s true Character and
Conduct at Bradford—on his alleged Opium-eating there.

When Branwell returned from London it was not without sincere satisfaction that his acquaintances welcomed their gifted and versatile friend back to Haworth, certain of whom induced him to become a freemason. Thus Branwell was brought into closer connection with the convivial circles of the village.

There was held at Haworth, at the time, 'The Lodge of the Three Graces.' In this lodge Branwell was proposed as a brother, and accepted on the 1st of February, 1836, initiated February the 29th, passed March the 28th, and raised April the 25th of that year, John Brown being the 'Worshipful Master.' Branwell was present at eleven meetings in 1836, the minutes of one of these—September the 18th—being fully entered by him. On December the 20th of the same year, he fulfilled the duties of 'Junior Warden;' and, at seven meetings of the lodge, from January the 16th to December the 11th, 1837, he was secretary, and entered the minutes. He also, on Christmas Day of the same year, officiated as organist. [23] In addition to his duties in connection with the Masonic Lodge, he likewise undertook the secretaryship of the local Temperance Society, of which he was a member.

Branwell's love of art had been too strong, and his interest in its practice too intense, to allow even such a check as that which his aspirations had received in the failure of the Academy project to finally discourage him. Hence it was, I suppose, when he had relinquished his place of usher that his passionate desire of becoming an artist, still cherished under disappointment, revived. He conceived, as the project of studying at the Royal Academy had not proved feasible, that, if he had a full course of instruction from Mr. Robinson, he could, in that way, qualify himself, perhaps as well, to adopt the profession of a portrait-painter, more valuable in those days, when photographers were not, than now; and Mr. Brontë, leaning to his son's wish, was induced to sanction the proposal, as it might provide Branwell with an alternative occupation to that of tutor, the only other that seemed open to him.

Mr. Robinson's charge, on the few occasions of his lessons at Haworth parsonage, had been two guineas for each visit. But it was now arranged that Branwell should receive instruction from the artist at his studio in Leeds. In this way he would not only have better opportunities of acquiring the art, but the cost would be much less. For this purpose, he stayed at an inn in Briggate, but occasionally took his master's pictures to Haworth to copy. Under this kind of tuition he continued for some months, when, having completed his studies, he resolved upon turning the instruction he had received, probably through the kindness of his aunt, to profitable account. With this professional intention, he engaged private apartments in Bradford, and took up his residence as a portrait-painter, under the interest of his mother's relative, the Rev. William Morgan, of Christ Church. Among others, he painted portraits of this gentleman, and of the Rev. Henry Heap, the vicar. For some months Branwell was successful in maintaining himself by these praiseworthy efforts; but it was scarcely to be expected that he could succeed sufficiently well in competition with the older and more experienced artists of the neighbourhood.

Among his other pictures, were portraits of Mrs. Kirby, his landlady, and her two children. One of these, a beautiful little girl, was his special favourite. At his frequent request, she dined with him in his private sitting-room, her pleasant smiles and cheerful prattling always charming him.

It may be mentioned here that, when Branwell had entered upon his studies under Mr. Robinson, he formed an acquaintance with a fellow-student, Mr. J. H. Thompson, who was a portrait-painter at Bradford. A close friendship grew up between them; and this artist, being more experienced than Branwell, gave, now and then, finishing touches to the productions of his young friend.

Soon after Branwell gave up his profession as an artist at Bradford, he wrote to Mr. Thompson, in reference to some misunderstanding which had arisen between himself and his landlady. The letter is dated from 'Haworth, May the 17th, 1839.'

'Dear Sir,

'Your last has made me resolve on a visit to you at Bradford, for certainly this train of misconceptions and delays must at last be put a stop to.

'I shall (Deo volente) be at the "Bull's Head" at two o'clock this afternoon (Friday), and *do* be there, or in Bradford, to give me your aid when I arrive!

'I am astonished at Mrs. Kirby. I have no pictures of hers to finish. But I said that, if I returned there, I would varnish three for her; and also I do not understand people who look on a kindness as a duty.

'Once more my heartfelt thanks to you for your consideration for one who has none for himself.

'YOURS FAITHFULLY,

'P. B. BRONTË.'

Mrs. Kirby had not been quite satisfied with the pictures before mentioned; but, on hearing Mr. Thompson's favourable opinion, she at once gave way. Although Branwell ceased his residence at Bradford for the reasons assigned, he afterwards painted portraits occasionally at Haworth; but also frequently visited his friends at the former place, having become acquainted with the poets and artists of the neighbourhood, as we shall presently see.

Miss Robinson has undertaken to draw Branwell's portrait at this juncture of his affairs, when she says he had attained the age of twenty years, though in fact he was twenty-two; and the following is the labour of her hands: 'He went to Bradford as a portrait-painter, and—so impressive is audacity—actually succeeded for some months in gaining a living there.... His tawny mane, his pose of untaught genius, his verses in the poet's corner of the paper could not for ever keep afloat this untaught and thriftless portrait-painter of twenty. Soon there came an end to his painting there. He disappeared from Bradford suddenly, heavily in debt, and was lost to sight until, unnerved, a drunkard, and an opium-eater, he came back to home and Emily at Haworth.' [24]

These statements are simply untrue. I have the positive information of one who knew Branwell in Leeds, and who resided in Bradford at the time when he was there, that he did not leave that town in debt; that he certainly was not a drunkard; and that, if he took anything at all, it was but occasionally, and then no more than the commonest custom would permit. I would rather believe—if all other evidence were wanting—the account of Branwell given by the friends who knew him personally, and who, at the moment in which I write, are still living on the spot where he exerted himself to gain a living by the labour of his own hands, than the unfair, unjust, and exaggerated charges quoted above. But Branwell's letter to his friend disposes at once of the assertion that he 'disappeared from Bradford suddenly, heavily in debt, and was lost to sight.' And, as to the statement that he was unnerved and a drunkard, one should surely rather accept the evidence of those who knew him, that he was, on the contrary, as they unhesitatingly say, 'a quiet, unassuming young man, retiring, and diffident, seeming rather of a passive nature, and delicate constitution, than otherwise.' And, moreover, his visits to Bradford, after he had given up his profession there, were frequent, for his literary tastes, his artistic pursuits, and his musical abilities had secured him many friends in that town. Assuredly the biographer of Emily has been very unfortunate, to say the least, in her account of Branwell's honest, upright, and honourable endeavour to make his living by the profession of art at Bradford.

Miss Robinson asserts that Branwell was an opium-eater 'of twenty,' in addition to the other baneful habits she ascribes to him. There is, however, no reliable evidence that, at this period of his life, he was any such thing; and, considering the fact that the biographer of Emily has assigned Branwell's art-practice at Bradford to a period subsequent to his tutorship at Broughton-in-Furness, one may, perhaps, be permitted to suspect that she is equally in error in her assertions as to his opium-eating so young. Branwell did, indeed, later, fall into the baneful habit, and suffered at times in consequence; but there is no reason to believe that he became wholly subject to it, or was greatly injured by the practice, either in mind or body. We can only surmise as to the original cause of his use of opium; but, when we consider the extraordinary fascination which De Quincey's wonderful book had for the younger generation of literary men of his day, we shall recognize that Branwell, who read the book, in all probability fell under its influence. Let us remember, moreover, that the young man's two sisters had died of consumption, and that De Quincey declares the use of the drug had saved him from the fate of his father who had fallen a victim to the same scourge. Lastly, it should not be forgotten that, in the first half of this century, the use of opium became, in some sort, fashionable amongst literary men, and that many admirers of De Quincey and Coleridge deemed that the practice had received a sufficient sanction. But the former of these writers had used the drug intermittently, and we have reason to believe that Branwell, who followed him, did likewise. Let us, then, imagine the young Brontë, revelling in the realm of the dreamy and impassioned, and hoping fondly that consumption might be driven away, resolving to try the effect of the 'dread agent of unimaginable pleasure and pain,' a proceeding from which many less brave would have shrunk. Branwell had doubtless read, in the 'Confessions of an English Opium-eater,' that the drug does not disorder the system; but gives tone, a sort of health, that might be natural if it were not for the means by which it is procured. He would believe that—in one under this magic spell, that is—'the diviner part of his nature is paramount, the moral affections are in a state of cloudless serenity; and high over all the great light of the majestic intellect.' Mrs. Gaskell describes the operation of opium upon herself. She says: 'I asked her' (Charlotte) 'whether she had ever taken opium, as the description of its effects, given in "Villette," was so exactly like what I had experienced—vivid and exaggerated presence of objects of which the outlines were indistinct, or lost in golden mist, etc.' [25] Branwell could not have tasted these stronger effects of the drug when he first made use of it; but it should be remembered that he several times recurred to the practice, and suffered the consequent pains and penalties.

After his portrait-painting at Bradford, he never again resided there, and it was about the period of his leaving that place that he began to see the artistic career he had chosen was a mistake, and he determined to give it up as a profession. Moreover, other influences, as we shall see, had been, and were still, at work upon him which caused him to turn once more to literature. From the period of his acquaintance with the drawing-masters, he had become associated with the literary as well as the artistic circles of the neighbourhood; and he anticipated the literary future of his sisters.

CHAPTER XII.

LITERARY INFLUENCES AND ASPIRATIONS.

New Inspiration of Poetry——, Scott, and Byron —to
Charlotte Brontë—Coleridge—Worthies of Yorkshire—of
the West-Riding—A. Watts—'s Literary Abilities.

In the early part of the present century, the spirit of poetry
began to make itself felt in quarters where previously it had
never been known. The pedantic affectation of the Della Cruscan
school gave place, in the works of a passionate lover of Nature like
Wordsworth, to a fresher and purer inspiration, that delighted
in familiar themes of domestic and rural beauty, which were
often both humble and obscure. It was Wordsworth, indeed,
who 'developed the theory of poetry,'—as Branwell Brontë well
knew—that has worked a greater change in literature than
has, perhaps, been known since the period of the Renaissance.
In his endeavour to solve the difficulty of 'fitting to metrical
arrangement a selection of the real language of men in a state
of vivid sensation,' Wordsworth had prepared the way for a
natural outburst of poetic feeling, occupied with familiar and
simple topics. The writers of the so-called 'Lake School' of poets,
and especially Wordsworth, Coleridge, and Southey, were, in
fact, the leaders of the new movement; and, speedily, responsive
to the free note of genius uncurbed, there arose from many an
unknown place in England the sweet sound of poetic voices
not heard before. At the same time, the touch of romanticism,
which was imparted by Scott and Byron, had a great influence
on many of the younger poets of the new school. It is evident, to

anyone who has studied the local literature of that time, that the works produced under such inspiration were often of great and permanent merit. Southey, writing to Charlotte Brontë in 1837, indeed says, 'Many volumes of poems are now published every year without attracting public attention, any one of which, if it had appeared half-a-century ago, would have obtained a high reputation for its author.'

Nowhere, probably, in England was the influence of the poets of Westmoreland felt more deeply than in the valleys of the West-Riding of Yorkshire. Indeed, a young publisher of that district, Mr. F. E. Bingley, had sufficient appreciation of genius, and enterprise enough, to bring him to Leeds for the purpose of publishing works from Hartley Coleridge's hand. The younger Coleridge—besides the prestige of his fathers name—had already become known as an occasional contributor to 'Blackwood's Magazine,' wherein first appeared his poem of 'Leonard and Susan,' so much admired. Mr. Bingley entered into an engagement to enable him to publish two volumes of poems, and a series of 'Biographical notices of the Worthies of Yorkshire and Lancashire,' which Hartley Coleridge was to write. One of the volumes of poems was issued from the press in 1833, and was well received. 'The Worthies' proceeded to the third number, forming an octavo volume of six hundred and thirty-two pages, when circumstances compelled Mr. Bingley to sell the remainders to another publisher, who issued a second edition of this well-known work, with a new title, in the year 1836. From the same press there came, in 1834, 'Cyril, a Poem in Four Cantos; and Minor Poems,' by George Wilson. C. F. Edgar, who was editor of the 'Yorkshire Literary Annual,' the first volume of which appeared in 1831, was also the author of a volume of poems, published by Mr. Bingley in the succeeding year; and other poetical works followed from the Leeds press.

But, in those days, there was scarcely a locality in the populous West-Riding of Yorkshire without its poet, and that poet, too, a man of no mean powers. Nicholson, the Airedale

poet, had, previously to the time of which I speak, published his
'Airedale, and other Poems,' and his 'Lyre of Ebor.' His poetical
talents were really excellent, and his versatility, and the happy
character of his effusions, made Nicholson very popular in the
West-Riding. He died in 1843. The gifted poet of Gargrave,
Robert Story, had published, in earlier years, many songs and
poems in the local papers; and he issued, in 1836, a volume,
entitled, 'The Magic Fountain.' This was followed, in 1838, by
'The Outlaw,' and by 'Love and Literature,' in the year 1842. This
poet was an ardent partizan of the Conservatives, and his lyrical
abilities were devoted with unflagging energy to their cause. His
'Songs and Poems,' and his 'Lyrical, and other Minor Poems,'
were subsequently published. His political songs were vigorous,
and his pastoral ones were redolent of pastures, meadows, and
moors, breathing all the freshness of nature in its happiest time.
Thomas Crossley, the 'Bard of Ovenden,' like Story, possessed of
lyrical talents of the highest order, was a frequent contributor to
the county papers; and he published, in 1837, an admirable and
delightful volume, entitled, 'The Flowers of Ebor.' In the same
year, William Dearden, the 'Bard of Caldene,' the possessor of
high gifts, published his 'Star-Seer; a Poem in Five Cantos,' which
was distinguished by great power, originality, and loftiness of
conception. It was largely influenced by the spirit of romanticism,
and flowed with the sweetest diction.

This also was the age of 'Souvenirs,' 'Keepsakes,' 'Forget-me-
nots,' and 'Annuals,' which sold very largely, and contained much
that was really good. Heath, the proprietor of the 'Keepsake,'
as we are told by Southey, sold fifteen thousand copies in one
year, and used four thousand yards of watered-silk for the next
issue; for these volumes were always resplendent in silk and gold.
Alaric A. Watts, who published, in 1822, his 'Poetical Sketches' (a
fourth edition of which, enlarged and exquisitely illustrated with
designs by Stothard and Nesfield, was required), became, in the
same year, editor of the 'Leeds Intelligencer,' which he conducted
with much spirit and ability. He afterwards established the

'Manchester Courier,' which he for some time edited, and was well-known in the northern shires. In 1828 and 1829 appeared his 'Poetical Album,' 'Scenes of Life, and Shades of Character,' in 1831; and from 1825 to 1834 he produced his 'Literary Souvenir; a Cabinet of Poetry and Romance,' with great and deserved success. It is more than likely that the great popularity of his venture led to the publication of 'The White Rose of York,' a similar volume, which was brought out at Halifax in the year 1834. This work was edited by George Hogarth, and, in addition to the authors already mentioned—who were, with the exception of Nicholson, the Airedale poet, and the Leeds authors, contributors to it— were F. C. Spencer, author of 'The Vale of Bolton,' a volume of poems; Henry Ingram, author of a volume entitled, 'Matilda'; Henry Martin, editor of the 'Halifax Express'; John Roby, author of 'The Traditions of Lancashire;' and others. There was also in the work a contribution, entitled 'Morley Hall,'—treating of a legend of the last-named county—by C. Peters, the subject of which also exercised the abilities of the author of 'The Flowers of Ebor'; and subsequently interested Branwell Brontë in a similar manner—his friend Leyland having modelled a scene from the story, in clay.

It is beyond question that these literary influences, which stirred the depths of feeling in Yorkshire, had a profound effect on the earlier writings of the Brontës, and probably were their original inspiration. All the local papers were filled with the news of the literary movement; and the busy brains in the parsonage of Haworth could not but be raised to emulation by the tidings. Branwell, especially, who knew personally many of the workers in the new field whom I have named, and was never so happy as when he could enjoy their company, was soon moved, in the midst of his art-aspirations, to partake in their literary labours. At this time, the tastes of the Brontës in this direction, and their progress in poetical and prose composition, began to inspire them with hopes and anticipations of the brightest character. From childhood their attempts at literary composition had formed, according to Charlotte herself, the highest stimulus, and one of the liveliest pleasures they had known. They began to find out that their genius was not artistic, but literary, and to pursue its bent with increasing ardour and the warmest interest.

It cannot be doubted that Branwell, greatly influenced, perhaps, by his sisters, or they, more probably, by him—for they ever regarded his genius as greater than their own—was soon employing his pen as often, and more successfully, than his pencil. Mr. Brontë's daughters were possessed largely of discriminating and critical powers, sufficient to enable them to judge accurately of the abilities of their brother; and Mrs. Gaskell allows that, to begin with, he was perhaps the greatest genius of this rare family, and this more even in a literary than in an artistic sense. Their favourable judgment was based on evidence they had before them. They were not ignorant of his poetical and prose compositions; and that these showed great beauty of thought and much felicity of expression, as well as considerable power, originality, and freshness of treatment, the evidences will appear in the subsequent pages.

CHAPTER XIII.

EARLY POEMS.

Branwell's Letter to Wordsworth, with Stanzas—upon
it—Reply—Tries Again—Interest in the Manchester and
Leeds Railway—'s Literary and Artistic Friends at Bradford
and Halifax—'s Works there—'s great Interest in them—
Verses—Mrs. Gaskell's Judgment on his Literary Abilities.

Branwell, even while working at art with great energy, was
not, as I have said, oblivious of his literary power. While,
however, the work of his sisters was to be conducted with great
earnestness of purpose, it was unfortunate that the scintillations
of Branwell's genius were too often fitful, erratic, and uncertain:
his mind, indeed, even at this time, was unstable.

It may be noted, as characteristic of all Mr. Brontë's children,
that, united with sterling gifts of intellectual power and literary
acumen, there was always some mistrust as to the merit of
their *own* productions, especially of poetical ones. They seem
to have felt themselves like travellers wandering in mist, or
struggling through a thicket, or toiling on devious paths with no
reliable information at hand, until they arrived at a point where
progress looked impossible, until they had obtained a guide in
whom they had confidence. It appeared, indeed, to the Brontës
that, without an opinion on their work, time might be altogether
wasted on what was unprofitable. Charlotte, therefore, in the
December of 1836, determined to submit some of her poems
to the judgment of Southey; and it would seem that she also
consulted Hartley Coleridge.

Before, however, Southey had answered his sister's letter, Branwell ventured, in a similar spirit, to address Wordsworth, for whose writings he had a great admiration. The following is his letter; and, although it has been previously published, it must not be omitted here. [26]

'HAWORTH, NEAR BRADFORD,

'YORKSHIRE, JANUARY 19TH, 1837.

'Sir,

'I most earnestly entreat you to read and pass your judgment upon what I have sent you, because from the day of my birth, to this the nineteenth year of my life, I have lived among secluded hills, where I could neither know what I was, or what I could do. I read for the same reason that I ate or drank—because it was a real craving of nature. I wrote on the same principle as I spoke—out of the impulse and feelings of the mind; nor could I help it, for what came, came out, and there was the end of it. For as to self-conceit, that could not receive food from flattery, since to this hour not half-a-dozen people in the world know that I have ever penned a line.

'But a change has taken place now, sir; and I am arrived at an age wherein I must do something for myself: the powers I possess must be exercised to a definite end, and as I don't know them myself I must ask of others what they are worth. Yet there is not one here to tell me; and still, if they are worthless, time will henceforth be too precious to be wasted on them.

'Do pardon me, sir, that I have ventured to come before one whose works I have most loved in our literature, and who most has been with me a divinity of the mind, laying before him one of my writings, and asking of him a judgment of its contents. I must come before some one from whose sentence there is no appeal; and such a one is he who has developed the theory of poetry as well as its practice, and both in such a way as to claim a place in the memory of a thousand years to come.

'My aim, sir, is to push out into the open world, and for this I trust not poetry alone—that might launch the vessel, but could not bear her on; sensible and scientific prose, bold and vigorous efforts in my walk in life, would give a further title to the notice of the world; and then, again, poetry ought to brighten and crown that name with glory; but nothing of all this can be ever begun without means, and as I don't possess these, I must in every shape strive to gain them. Surely, in this day, when there is not a *writing* poet worth a sixpence, the field must be open, if a better man can step forward.

'What I send you is the Prefatory Scene of a much longer subject, in which I have striven to develop strong passions and weak principles struggling with a high imagination and acute feelings, till, as youth hardens towards old age, evil deeds and short enjoyments end in mental misery and bodily ruin. Now, to send you the whole of this would be a mock upon your patience; what you see, does not even pretend to be more than the description of an imaginative child. But read it, sir; and, as you would hold a light to one in utter darkness—as you value your own kind-heartedness—*return* me an *answer*, if but one word, telling me whether I should write on, or write no more. Forgive undue warmth, because my feelings in this matter cannot be cool; and believe me, sir, with deep respect,

'YOUR REALLY HUMBLE SERVANT,

'P. B. BRONTË.'

Mrs. Gaskell gives the following six stanzas, which are about a third of the whole, and declares them not to be the worst part of the composition:—

'So where He reigns in glory bright,
Above those starry skies of night,
Amid His Paradise of light,
   Oh, why may I not be?

'Oft when awake on Christmas morn,
In sleepless twilight laid forlorn,
Strange thoughts have o'er my mind been borne
   How He has died for me.

'And oft, within my chamber lying,
Have I awaked myself with crying,
From dreams, where I beheld Him dying
   Upon the accursed tree.

'And often has my mother said,
While on her lap I laid my head,
She feared for time I was not made,
   But for Eternity.

'So "I can read my title clear
To mansions in the skies,
And let me bid farewell to fear,
   And wipe my weeping eyes."

'I'll lay me down on this marble stone,
And set the world aside,

To see upon her ebon throne
   The Moon in glory ride.'

Branwell's letter to Wordsworth is, for the most part, well written, and breathes an eager spirit, which shows the anxiety he was under to know the opinion of a high and competent judge as to how he stood with the Nine. It tells us the ardour with which he read and wrote, the ambitious turn of his mind, and the special aims which he then had in the literary world. But the verses, although imbued with a fervent spirit of early piety, were such as Wordsworth could not justly review without giving discouragement, and it seems probable he preferred to keep silence rather than, by an open avowal, to give pain—if pain must be given—as the lesser evil of the two. Or, perhaps, he took amiss the ready frankness and apparent self-esteem which, notwithstanding the disavowal, would probably seem present to him in the letter of the young stranger who addressed him, without sending any evidence of the powers of which he expressed himself so confidently. But, at any rate, Mrs. Gaskell informs us that the letter and verses were preserved by the poet till the Brontës became celebrated, and that he gave the communication to his friend, Mr. Quillinan, in 1850, when the real name of 'Currer Bell' became known.

It must not be overlooked that, in the verses which Mrs. Gaskell has printed, we have no opportunity of studying Branwell's dramatic powers, which apparently found scope in the poem he had written. In them is no development of the effect of the passionate feelings which Branwell describes: 'struggling with a high imagination and acute feelings,' and ending 'in mental misery and bodily ruin.'

However, discouraged by long waiting, or assisted by friendly advice and criticism, he toiled on in silence at his literary work, as he did at art. The year 1837 turned out an important one for Charlotte. In March, she at last received the answer from Southey, which she considered a 'little stringent,' and from which she declared she had derived good. She says, in her reply to the Laureate, 'I trust I shall never more feel ambitious to see my name in print…. That letter is consecrated; no one shall ever see it, but papa, and my brother and my sisters.'

It would seem that Branwell, notwithstanding the failure of his first venture with Wordsworth, tried again, at a later date, with some other, and more matured, compositions, which he submitted to that poet and to Hartley Coleridge, 'who both,' says Mrs. Gaskell, 'expressed kind and laudatory opinions.' But, perhaps, the fact that, to the letter quoted above, Wordsworth sent no answer, and did not tell him whether he should 'write on, or write no more,' discouraged Branwell for a time; and he may have been led to suspect that his productions were worthless, and that time might 'henceforth be too precious to be wasted upon them.' In this way, perhaps, he was induced to turn with greater energy to his profession of art, as a means of getting on, of which I spoke in a former chapter, though we shall see that he did not abandon his literary work.

Branwell also now found opportunities of making himself acquainted with the grand and wild scenery of the mountainous borders of the counties of York and Lancaster, a wider district than his sisters could well survey.

The Manchester and Leeds Railway was, at the time, in course of construction below Littleborough, passing through the picturesque and romantic vale of Todmorden. Branwell became greatly interested in the work; and as stores, and other things for the completion of the line to Hebden Bridge, were forwarded from Littleborough by canal, having been previously sent to that place from Manchester by train, he soon ingratiated himself with the boatmen, and was frequently seen in their boats. It was on one of these occasions that Mr. Woolven, previously mentioned, who was officially employed on the works, recognized at once the clever young man who had surprised the company at the 'Castle Tavern,' Holborn, and entered into conversation with him. These incidents led to a friendly intercourse between them, which continued for some years.

Among his Bradford acquaintances, Branwell numbered, in addition to Geller, the mezzotinto-engraver, previously mentioned, Wilson Anderson, an admirable landscape-painter, whose productions are valued as truthful pictures of the places they represent, and on account of the skilfulness of their manipulation and colouring; and also Richard Waller, a well-known and excellent portrait-painter. To these may be added Edward Collinson, a local poet; Robert Story; and John James, the future historian of Bradford. All these were personal acquaintances of Branwell, as well as of Leyland, and the intercourse between them was frequent. For more than twenty years a party of these friends was accustomed to meet, from time to time, at the 'George Hotel,' Bradford, under the auspices of Miss Rennie, who greatly prided herself on seeing at her house, in their hours of leisure, the artistic and literary celebrities of the neighbourhood. Leyland was at Halifax, being there to erect certain monuments, which he had executed in London for various patrons in his native town. While there, he modelled, in the upper room of an ancient house, his colossal group of 'African Bloodhounds,' his model being a living specimen of the breed; and the group, which was exhibited in London, was favourably noticed. Landseer regarded it as the 'noblest modern work of its kind.' It is now in the Salford Museum. The progress of this group intensely interested Branwell and his Bradford friends; and they frequently visited Leyland's temporary studio. It also formed the subject of a poem by Dearden. [27] Finding this studio of insufficient height for a great work he contemplated—a colossal group of 'Thracian Falconers'—Leyland afterwards took a suitable place in another part of the town, which, likewise, became a meeting-place of the local *literati*. The new work was to consist of three figures, the centre one being seated, and having upon his right fore-finger a hawk; while his left hand rested on the shoulder of a youth just roused, as if by some sudden sound; and, on his right, was a similar youth, half-recumbent, and also in a listening attitude. The centre figure was alone completed, and is now in the Salford Museum.

Branwell, on his visits to the artist's studio, often lamented the dissipation of his high artistic hopes, and confessed that he saw with pain how misplaced his confidence in his own powers had been. But the sculptor was a poet also, and thus Branwell and he worked in the same field. Many of Leyland's poems were published in the Yorkshire papers, and also in the 'Morning Chronicle,' and were always considered to be of true poetic excellence. Branwell relied much on the artist's judgment in literary matters, and often submitted his productions to him.

Although Brontë had, as we have seen, abandoned the hope of a high artistic career, he still clung to the practice of portrait-painting, and this gave him leisure to court the muse. The following are the earliest of his poems, of which the MSS. are in my possession; and these are fragments only. The first is a verse of eleven lines, dated January 23rd, 1838, which originally concluded a poem of sixty;—

'There's many a grief to shade the scene,
    And hide the starry skies;
But all such clouds that intervene
    From mortal life arise.
And—may I smile—O God! to see
Their storms of sorrow beat on me,
    When I so surely know
That Thou, the while, art shining on;
That I, at last, when they are gone,
Shall see the glories of Thy throne,
    So far more bright than now.'

This fragment, written by Branwell at the age of twenty-one, is characteristic of the early tone of his mind. His naturally amiable and susceptible disposition had soon become imbued with the spirit of Christian piety which surrounded his life. He was, too, at the time, full of noble impulses and high aspirations; but the shade of melancholy implanted in his constitution had begun to influence his writings. The following, which is the beginning of another poem, must have been written in some such thoughtful mood, though the title is not borne out in the portion I am able to give.

DEATH TRIUMPHANT.

May, 1838.

'Oh! on this first bright Mayday morn,
    That seems to change our earth to Heaven,
May my own bitter thoughts be borne,
    With the wild winter it has driven!
Like this earth, may my mind be made
    To feel the freshness round me spreading,
    No other aid to rouse it needing
Than thy glad light, so long delayed.
    Sweet woodland sunshine!—none but thee
    Can wake the joys of memory,
Which seemed decaying, as all decayed.

'O! may they bud, as thou dost now,
    With promise of a summer near!
Nay—let me feel my weary brow—
    Where are the ringlets wreathing there?
Why does the hand that shades it tremble?
    Why do these limbs, so languid, shun
    Their walk beneath the morning sun?
Ah, mortal Self! couldst thou dissemble
    Like Sister-Soul! But forms refuse

The real and unreal to confuse.
But, with caprice of fancy, She
Joins things long past with things to be,
Till even I doubt if I have told
    My tale of woes and wonders o'er,
Or think Her magic can unfold
    A phantom path of joys before—
Or, laid beneath this Mayday blaze—
Ask, "Live I o'er departed days?"
Am I the child by Gambia's side,
Beneath its woodlands waving wide?
Have I the footsteps bounding free,
The happy laugh of infancy?'

In this beautiful fragment we have the first passionate out-pouring of the self-imposed woes, which, proceeding from within, were thereafter to overspread and tincture with darkest colours every thought of Branwell's mind. We see him here for a moment, standing in incipient melancholia, in what appears to him to be a desert of mental despondency; but, turning back with a fond affection for the past, and recalling, in plaintive words, the joys of 'departed days.' He seems here, indeed, to seek in the mysteries of the soul those pleasures and hopes which his mortal self cannot afford him. Branwell never appears to have forgotten, as I have previously suggested, the sad circumstances of the death of his sisters; and his solitary broodings over these visitations gave a morbid tone to his writings. It was in 1838 that he adopted the pseudonym of 'Northangerland.' His earlier poems, although occasionally showing some power, were not sufficiently gifted to add to the lustre of Brontë literature.

Mrs. Gaskell, alluding to Branwell's literary abilities about this time, says: 'In a fragment of one of his manuscripts which I have read, there is a justness and felicity of expression which is very striking. It is the beginning of a tale, and the actors in it are drawn with much of the grace of characteristic portrait-painting, in perfectly pure and simple language, which distinguishes so many of Addison's papers in the "Spectator." The fragment is too short to afford the means of judging whether he had much dramatic talent, as the persons of the story are not thrown into conversation. But, altogether, the elegance and composure of style are such as one would not have expected from this vehement and ill-fated young man. 'He had,' continues Mrs. Gaskell, 'a stronger desire for literary fame burning in his heart than even that which occasionally flashed up in his sisters'.' She says also that, 'He tried various outlets for his talents ... and he frequently contributed verses to the "Leeds Mercury."' The latter statement, however, is incorrect, for nothing of Branwell's appears in that journal.

CHAPTER XIV.

POEMS ON 'CAROLINE.'

The Poetical bent of Branwell's Genius—'Caroline's
Prayer'—'On Caroline'—'Caroline'—of these Early
Effusions.

While Branwell was occupying his leisure as stated in the
last chapter, and otherwise employing himself in a desultory
way, he pursued the poetic bent of his genius, and sought the
improvement of his diction and verse. Among the earliest of his
poetical productions, the following are, perhaps, the best. They
are distinguished by a similar train of thought and reflection, and
by similar sentiments of piety and devotion, as also by the same
gloom and sadness of mood, which pervade the poems of his
sisters. Indeed, without knowing they were actually Branwell's,
we might easily believe them to be from the pen of Charlotte,
Emily, or Anne.

The three following poetical essays are on 'Caroline,' under
which name Branwell indicates his sister Maria; and, in two of
them, he records his reminiscences of her death and funeral
obsequies. The first of the three, which he has framed in the
sentiments and words of a child, is entitled:

CAROLINE'S PRAYER,

OR THE CHANGE FROM CHILDHOOD TO WOMANHOOD.

'My Father, and my childhood's guide!
   If oft I've wandered far from Thee;
E'en though Thine only Son has died
   To save from death a child like me;

'O! still—to Thee when turns my heart
   In hours of sadness, frequent now—
Be Thou the God that once Thou wert,
   And calm my breast, and clear my brow.

'I'm now no more a little child
   O'ershadowed by Thy mighty wing;
My very dreams seem now more wild
   Than those my slumbers used to bring.

'I further see—I deeper feel—
   With hope more warm, but heart less mild;
And former things new shapes reveal,
   All strangely brightened or despoiled.

'I'm entering on Life's open tide;
   So—farewell childhood's shores divine!
And, oh, my Father, deign to guide,
   Through these wide waters, Caroline!'

The second is:

ON CAROLINE.

'The light of thy ancestral hall,
    Thy Caroline, no longer smiles:
She has changed her palace for a pall,
    Her garden walks for minster aisles:
Eternal sleep has stilled her breast
    Where peace and pleasure made their shrine;
Her golden head has sunk to rest—
    Oh, would that rest made calmer mine!

'To thee, while watching o'er the bed
    Where, mute and motionless, she lay,
How slow the midnight moments sped!
    How void of sunlight woke the day!
Nor ope'd her eyes to morning's beam,
    Though all around thee woke to her;
Nor broke thy raven-pinioned dream
    Of coffin, shroud, and sepulchre.

'Why beats thy breast when hers is still?
    Why linger'st thou when she is gone?
Hop'st thou to light on good or ill?
    To find companionship alone?
Perhaps thou think'st the churchyard stone
    Can hide past smiles and bury sighs:
That Memory, with her soul, has flown;
    That thou canst leave her where she lies.

'No! joy *itself* is but a shade,
    So well may its remembrance die;
But cares, life's conquerors, never fade,
    So strong is their reality!
Thou may'st forget the day which gave

That child of beauty to thy side,
But not the moment when the grave
    Took back again thy borrowed bride.'

Here Branwell, though he has changed the form of expression and the circumstance of the loss, is still occupied with the same theme of family bereavement, with which Charlotte herself was so much impressed.

The following was intended as the first canto of a long poem. It also is entitled, 'Caroline;' and is the soliloquy of one 'Harriet,' who mourns for her sister, the subject of the poem, calling to mind her early recollection of the death and funeral of the departed one. It is extremely probable that Branwell made 'Harriet' a vehicle of expression for Charlotte or Emily, as he had adopted the name of 'Caroline' for Maria.

CAROLINE.

'Calm and clear the day declining,
    Lends its brightness to the air,
With a slanted sunlight shining,
    Mixed with shadows stretching far:
Slow the river pales its glancing,
Soft its waters cease their dancing,
As the hush of eve advancing
    Tells our toils that rest is near.

'Why is such a silence given
    To this summer day's decay?
Does our earth feel aught of Heaven?
    Can the voice of Nature pray?
And when daylight's toils are done,
Beneath its mighty Maker's throne.

Can it, for noontide sunshine gone,
  Its debt with smiles repay?

'Quiet airs of sacred gladness
  Breathing through these woodlands wild,
O'er the whirl of mortal madness
  Spread the slumbers of a child:
These surrounding sweeps of trees
Swaying to the evening breeze,
With a voice like distant seas,
  Making music mild.

'Woodchurch Hall above them lowering
  Dark against the pearly sky,
With its clustered chimneys towering,
  Wakes the wind while passing by:
And in old ancestral glory,
Round that scene of ancient story,
All its oak-trees, huge and hoary,
  Wave their boughs on high.

"Mid those gables there is one—
  The soonest dark when day is gone—
Which, when autumn winds are strongest,
  Moans the most and echoes longest.
There—with her curls like sunset air,
Like it all balmy, bright, and fair—
Sits Harriet, with her cheek reclined
  On arm as white as mountain snow;
While, with a bursting swell, her mind
  Fills with thoughts of "Long Ago."

'As from yon spire a funeral bell,
  Wafting through heaven its mourning knell,
Warns man that life's uncertain day

131

Like lifeless Nature's must decay;
And tells her that the warning deep
Speaks where her own forefathers sleep,
And where destruction makes a prey
    Of what was once this world to her,
But which—like other gods of clay—
    Has cheated its blind worshipper:
With swelling breast and shining eyes
That seem to chide the thoughtless skies,
She strives in words to find relief
For long-pent thoughts of mellowed grief.

"'Time's clouds roll back, and memory's light
Bursts suddenly upon my sight;
For thoughts, which words could never tell,
Find utterance in that funeral bell.
My heart, this eve, seemed full of feeling,
Yet nothing clear to me revealing;
Sounding in breathings undefined
Æolian music to my mind:
    Then strikes that bell, and all subsides
Into a harmony, which glides
As sweet and solemn as the dream
Of a remembered funeral hymn.
    This scene seemed like the magic glass,
Which bore upon its clouded face
Strange shadows that deceived the eye
With forms defined uncertainly;
That Bell is old Agrippa's wand,
Which parts the clouds on either hand,
And shows the pictured forms of doom
Momently brightening through the gloom:
Yes—shows a scene of bygone years—
Opens a fount of sealed-up tears—
And wakens memory's pensive thought

To visions sleeping—not forgot.
It brings me back a summer's day,
Shedding like this its parting ray,
With skies as shining and serene,
And hills as blue, and groves as green.

'"Ah, well I recollect that hour,
    When I sat, gazing, just as now,
Toward that ivy-mantled tower
    Among these flowers which wave below!
No—not these flowers—they're long since dead,
    And flowers have budded, bloomed, and gone,
Since those were plucked which gird the head
    Laid underneath yon churchyard stone!
I stooped to pluck a rose that grew
    Beside this window, waving then;
But back my little hand withdrew,
    From some reproof of inward pain;
For *she who loved it* was not there
    To check me with her dove-like eye,
And something bid my heart forbear
    Her favourite rosebud to destroy.
Was it that bell—that funeral bell,
    Sullenly sounding on the wind?
Was it that melancholy knell
    Which first to sorrow woke my mind?
I looked upon my mourning dress
    Till my heart beat with childish fear,
And—frightened at my loneliness—
    I watched, some well-known sound to hear.
But all without lay silent in
    The sunny hush of afternoon,
And only muffled steps within
    Passed slowly and sedately on.
I well can recollect the awe

With which I hastened to depart;
   And, as I ran, the instinctive start
With which my mother's form I saw,
Arrayed in black, with pallid face,
   And cheeks and 'kerchief wet with tears,
As down she stooped to kiss my face
   And quiet my uncertain fears.

"'She led me, in her mourning hood,
   Through voiceless galleries, to a room,
'Neath whose black hangings crowded stood,
   With downcast eyes and brows of gloom,
My known relations; while—with head
Declining o'er my sister's bed—
My father's stern eye dropt a tear
Upon the coffin resting there.
My mother lifted me to see
What might within that coffin be;
And, to this moment, I can feel
The voiceless gasp—the sickening chill—
With which I hid my whitened face
In the dear folds of her embrace;
For hardly dared I turn my head
Lest its wet eyes should view that bed.
   'But, Harriet,' said my mother mild,
'Look at *your* sister and my child
One moment, ere her form be hid
For ever 'neath its coffin lid!'
   I heard the appeal, and answered too;
For down I bent to bid adieu.
But, as I looked, forgot affright
In mild and magical delight.

"'There lay she then, as now she lies—
   For not a limb has moved since then—

In dreamless slumber closed, those eyes
    That never more might wake again.
She lay, as I had seen her lie
    On many a happy night before,
When I was humbly kneeling by—
    Whom she was teaching to adore:
Oh, just as when by her I prayed,
    And she to heaven sent up my prayer,
She lay with flowers about her head—
    Though formal grave-clothes hid her hair!
Still did her lips the smile retain
    Which parted them when hope was high,
Still seemed her brow as smoothed from pain
    As when all thought she could not die.
And, though her bed looked cramped and strange,
    Her *too* bright cheek all faded now,
My young eyes scarcely saw a change
    From hours when moonlight paled her brow.
And yet I felt—and scarce could speak—
    A chilly face, a faltering breath,
When my hand touched the marble cheek
    Which lay so passively beneath.
In fright I gasped, 'Speak, Caroline!'
    And bade my sister to arise;
But answered not her voice to mine,
    Nor ope'd her sleeping eyes.
I turned toward my mother then
    And prayed on her to call;
But, though she strove to hide her pain,
    It forced her tears to fall.
She pressed me to her aching breast
    As if her heart would break,
And bent in silence o'er the rest
    Of one she could not wake:
The rest of one, whose vanished years

Her soul had watched in vain;
The end of mother's hopes and fears,
 And happiness and pain.

'"They came—they pressed the coffin lid
 Above my Caroline,
And then, I felt, for ever hid
 My sister's face from mine!
There was one moment's wildered start—
 One pang remembered well—
When first from my unhardened heart
 The tears of anguish fell:
That swell of thought which seemed to fill
 The bursting heart, the gushing eye,
While fades all *present* good or ill
 Before the shades of things gone by.
All else seems blank—the mourning march,
 The proud parade of woe,
The passage 'neath the churchyard arch,
 The crowd that met the show.
My place or thoughts amid the train
I strive to recollect, in vain—
 I could not think or see:
I cared not whither I was borne:
And only felt that death had torn
 My Caroline from me.

'"Slowly and sadly, o'er her grave,
The organ peals its passing stave,
And, to its last dark dwelling-place,
 The corpse attending mourners bear,
While, o'er it bending, many a face
 'Mongst young companions shows a tear.
I think I glanced toward the crowd
 That stood in musing silence by,

And even now I hear the sound
   Of some one's voice amongst them cry—
'I am the Resurrection and the Life—
   He who believes in me shall never die!'

"'Long years have never worn away
The unnatural strangeness of that day,
When I beheld—upon the plate
Of grim death's mockery of state—
That well-known word, that long-loved name,
Now but remembered like the dream
Of half-forgotten hymns divine,
My sister's name—my Caroline!
   Down, down, they lowered her, sad and slow,
Into her narrow house below:
And deep, indeed, appeared to be
That one glimpse of eternity,
Where, cut from life, corruption lay,
Where beauty soon should turn to clay!
Though scarcely conscious, hotly fell
The drops that spoke my last farewell;
And wild my sob, when hollow rung
The first cold clod above her flung,
When glitter was to turn to rust,
'Ashes to ashes, dust to dust!'

"'How bitter seemed that moment when,
   Earth's ceremonies o'er,
We from the filled grave turned again
   To leave her evermore;
And, when emerging from the cold
   Of damp, sepulchral air,
As I turned, listless to behold
   The evening fresh and fair,
How sadly seemed to smile the face

Of the descending sun!
How seemed as if his latest race
   Were with that evening run!
There sank his orb behind the grove
   Of my ancestral home,
With heaven's unbounded vault above
   To canopy his tomb.
Yet lingering sadly and serene,
   As for his last farewell,
To shine upon those wild woods green
   O'er which he'd loved to dwell.

"'I lost him, and the silent room,
   Where soon at rest I lay,
Began to darken, 'neath the gloom
   Of twilight's dull decay;
So, sobbing as my heart would break,
   And blind with gushing eyes,
Hours seemed whole nights to me awake,
   And day as 'twould not rise.
I almost prayed that I might die—
   But then the thought would come
That, if I did, my corpse must lie
   In yonder dismal tomb;
Until, methought, I saw its stone,
   By moonshine glistening clear,
While Caroline's bright form alone
   Kept silent watching there:
All white with angel's wings she seemed,
   And indistinct to see;
But when the unclouded moonlight beamed
   I saw her beckon me,
And fade, thus beckoning, while the wind
   Around that midnight wall,
To me—now lingering years behind—

Seemed then my sister's call!

'"And thus it brought me back the hours
    When we, at rest together,
Used to lie listening to the showers
    Of wild December weather;
Which, when, as oft, they woke in her
    The chords of inward thought,
Would fill with pictures that wild air,
    From far off memories brought;
So, while I lay, I heard again
    Her silver-sounding tongue,
Rehearsing some remembered strain
    Of old times long agone!
And, flashed across my spirit's sight,
    What she had often told me—
When, laid awake on Christmas night,
    Her sheltering arms would fold me—
About that midnight-seeming day,
    Whose gloom o'er Calvary thrown,
Showed trembling Nature's deep dismay
    At what her sons had done:
When sacred Salem's murky air
    Was riven with the cry,
Which told the world how mortals dare
    The Immortal crucify;
When those who, sorrowing, sat afar,
    With aching heart and eye,
Beheld their great Redeemer there,
    'Mid sneers and scoffings die;
When all His earthly vigour fled,
When thirsty faintness bowed His head,
When His pale limbs were moistened o'er
With deathly dews and dripping gore,
When quivered all His worn-out frame,

As Death, triumphant, quenched life's flame,
When upward gazed His glazing eyes
To those tremendous-seeming skies,
When burst His cry of agony—
'My God!—my God!—hast Thou forsaken me!'
   My youthful feelings startled then,
As if the temple, rent in twain,
Horribly pealing on my ear
With its deep thunder note of fear,
Wrapping the world in general gloom,
As if her God's were Nature's tomb;
While sheeted ghosts before my gaze
Passed, flitting 'mid the dreary maze,
As if rejoicing at the day
When death—their king—o'er Heaven had sway.
   In glistening charnel damps arrayed,
They seemed to gibber round my head,
Through night's drear void directing me
Toward still and solemn Calvary,
Where gleamed that cross with steady shine
Around the thorn-crowned head divine—
A flaming cross—a beacon light
To this world's universal night!
It seemed to shine with such a glow,
And through my spirit piercing so,
That, pantingly, I strove to cry
For her, whom I thought slumbered by,
And hide me from that awful shine
In the embrace of Caroline!
   I wakened in the attempt—'twas day;
The troubled dream had fled away;
'Twas day—and I, alone, was laid
In that great room and stately bed;
No Caroline beside me! Wide
And unrelenting swept the tide

Of death 'twixt her and me!"
                    There paused
Sweet Harriet's voice, for such thoughts caused—'

This poem springs from the deepest feelings, and from sorrows the most poignant. The respective images, tinctured with grief and despondency, pass before us with weird and vivid reality; and many of the passages are imbued with great tenderness, beauty, and pathos. The painful, and, perhaps, too morbid intensity of some of the pictures, whether of dreams or realities, is painted here with the skill of no common artist, whatever youthful defects may be observed in the composition. The poem is one more notable for tender sweetness than any other that remains from Branwell; but it lacks in places the vigour and power of his later compositions, and is, in several parts, of unequal merit. In the earlier portion of it, where he assumes the iambic measure, it is not difficult to perceive the influence of Byron on his diction. In this work Branwell again recurs to the time when tears of anguish flowed from his yet 'unhardened heart,' whose present woes are forgotten in the swelling thoughts of 'things gone by.' We recognize with what pathetic feeling he paints in Caroline all the qualities of instructress, guardian, and friend, which had characterized his sister Maria. Long afterwards Charlotte Brontë, inspired by similar feelings, devoted the first chapters of 'Jane Eyre' to a delineation, in the character of Helen Burns, of the disposition of her dead sister, whose death, a few days after her return from Cowan Bridge, she could scarcely ever either forget or forgive.

CHAPTER XV.

EVENTS AT THE PARSONAGE.

Charlotte's first Offer of Marriage—Her Remarks
concerning it—A second Offer Declined—a Governess—
Moralizes upon it—obtains a Situation—to Her—Leaves
it—takes Pleasure in Scenery—Visits Liverpool with his
Friends—goes to Easton—at Haworth—Visits to the
Parsonage—Public Meetings on Church Rates—'s Attempt
at a Richardsonian Novel—sends the Commencement of it
to Wordsworth for his Opinion—receives an
Appointment as Private Tutor.

After the return of Charlotte and Anne from Dewsbury Moor,
whither Miss Wooler had removed her school, the three sisters
were at home together for some months, and, in this happy,
unrestrained intercourse, with their literary relaxations and
their plans for the future, Charlotte's mind expanded, and her
strength returned. There was Branwell, too, to think about; his
venture at Bradford and his progress with his portraits. Then
they would have to go and see the likeness of Mr. Morgan; and,
on such occasions, Branwell would have much to say of art
and literature, and, acquaintances. But Branwell was usually
at Haworth on Sundays, and then he would hear of Charlotte's
visits to her friends, and her adventures on these occasions. It
was shortly before the date of Branwell's return from Bradford,
in the spring of 1839, that Charlotte received her first offer
of marriage. A young clergyman, who had, as Mrs. Gaskell
thought, some resemblance to the St. John in the last volume

of 'Jane Eyre,' had evidently been attracted by Charlotte Brontë; but matrimony does not seem, at the time, to have seriously entered into her thoughts. In some respects the proposal might have had strong temptations for her, and she thought how happy her married life might be. However, it was not the way with Charlotte Brontë to take the path of smoothness and comfort, and leave the thorny one untrod; and she asked herself if she loved the clergyman in question as much as a woman should love her husband, and whether she was the one best qualified to make him happy. 'Alas!' she says, 'my conscience answered "No" to both these questions.' She knew very well that she had a 'kindly leaning' towards him, but this was not enough for her, for it was impossible that she could ever feel for him such an intense attachment as would make her sacrifice her life for him. Short of such a devotion awakened in herself, she would never marry anyone. Her comment is characteristic: 'Ten to one I shall never have the chance again; but *n'importe.*'

Charlotte Brontë felt that there was a want of sympathy between the young clergyman and herself, for he was a 'grave, quiet young man;' and she knew that he would be startled, and would think her a wild, romantic enthusiast, when she showed her character, and laughed, and satirized, and said whatever came into her head. Nor was her next offer any more to her taste; for, within a few months, a neighbouring curate, a young Irishman, fresh from the Dublin University, made her a proposal. The circumstance amused Charlotte, for it was, on his part, a case of love at first sight. He came with his vicar to be introduced to the family, and was speedily struck with Mr. Brontë's daughter. Charlotte was never troubled at home with the *mauvaise honte* that troubled her abroad; and so she talked and jested with the clergyman, and was much amused at the originality of his character. A pleasant afternoon was spent, for he made himself at home, after the fashion of his countrymen, and was witty, lively, ardent, and clever; but, withal, wanting in the dignity and discretion of an Englishman. As the evening drew on, Charlotte was not much pleased with the spice of Hibernian flattery with which he began to season his discourse, and, as she expresses it, she 'cooled a little.' The vicar and his curate went away; but what was Charlotte's astonishment to receive a letter next morning from the latter containing a proposal of marriage, and filled with ardent expressions of devotion! 'I hope you are laughing heartily,' she says to her friend. 'This is not like one of my adventures, is it? It more nearly resembles Martha's. I am certainly doomed to be an old maid. Never mind. I have made up my mind to that fate ever since I was twelve years old. Well! thought I, I have heard of love at first sight, but this beats all! I leave you to guess what my answer would be, convinced that you will not do me the injustice of guessing wrong.'

Although the married state does not appear, from Charlotte's letters at this time, to have had many attractions for her, we know, from those she wrote later, and, perhaps, more than all from the concluding chapters of 'Jane Eyre,' that she could enter into the joys and sacrifices of domestic life, that she had a correct view of the affections, and knew how to appreciate conjugal love at its true value. But, in the present instances—although, at a later period of her life, when she was on the Continent, she is believed to have felt the full force of that 'passion of the heart' which those about whom she wrote had failed to evoke—she declined to sever herself from the contented circumstances that surrounded her, and in which she was mistress, for a condition of doubtful peace and certain obedience. Charlotte's decision was not discordant with the feelings of her family; for, as she had determined to continue at home, their plans for the future would not be disconcerted.

Anne was now resolved on making a trial of the life of a governess for herself, she having completed her education, and being wishful to exert herself as her sisters had done. Inquiries were made, and at length a situation was obtained. Anne continued in this kind of employment during the next six years, and it was her experience that suggested to her the subject of her first novel, 'Agnes Grey.' If we may suppose that she has recounted her own experience at this time, where her heroine describes the circumstances of her preparation and departure for her first situation, it would appear that she had some difficulty in convincing her friends of the wisdom of her purpose. Agnes Grey says, after she has made the suggestion to her family:

'I was silenced for that day, and for many succeeding ones; but still I did not wholly relinquish my darling scheme. Mary got her drawing materials, and steadily set to work. I got mine too; but, while I drew, I thought of other things. How delightful it would be to be a governess! To go out into the world; to enter upon a new life; to act for myself; to exercise my unused faculties; to try my unknown powers; to earn my own maintenance, and something to comfort and help my father, mother, and sister, besides exonerating them from the provision of my food and clothing; to show papa what his little Agnes could do; to convince mamma and Mary that I was not quite the helpless, thoughtless being they supposed. And then, how charming to be entrusted with the care and education of children! Whatever others said, I felt I was fully competent to the task: the clear remembrance of my own thoughts in early childhood would be a surer guide than the instructions of the most mature adviser. I had but to turn from my little pupils to myself at their age, and I should know at once how to win their confidence and affections; how to waken the contrition of the erring; how to embolden the timid and console the afflicted; how to make virtue practicable, instruction desirable, and religion lively and comprehensible.' [28]

Anne Brontë was of a milder and more cheerful temperament than her sisters; she had not the fire, the morbid feeling, or the mental force that characterized Charlotte, yet she had more of the initiatory faculty than she had hitherto received credit for. But her gentle nature, her confiding piety, her more equable temper, enabled her to succeed better in the circumstances she had chosen. She had her troubles, her timidity, and her diffidence to contend with, but she made life supportable and even happy.

'Agnes Grey' thus speaks of her departure, which we cannot doubt is the experience of Anne Brontë:

'Some weeks more were yet to be devoted to preparation. How long, how tedious those weeks appeared to me! Yet they were happy ones in the main, full of bright hopes and ardent expectations. With what peculiar pleasure I assisted at the making of my new clothes, and, subsequently, the packing of my trunks! But there was a feeling of bitterness mingling with the latter occupation too; and when it was done—when all was ready for my departure on the morrow, and the last night at home approached—a sudden anguish seemed to swell my heart. My dear friends looked sad, and spoke so very kindly, that I could scarcely keep my heart from overflowing; but I still affected to be gay. I had taken my last ramble with Mary on the moors, my last walk in the garden and round the house ... I had played my last tune on the old piano, and sung my last song to papa, not the last, I hoped, but the last for what appeared to me a very long time.' [29]

Charlotte and Emily made themselves busy in assisting Anne with her preparations for departure, and they were very sad and apprehensive when she left them on Monday, April 15th, 1839. She went alone, at her own wish, thinking she could manage better if left to her own resources, and when her failings were unwitnessed by those whose hopes she wished to sustain. However, she wrote, expressing satisfaction with the place she had secured, for the lady of the house was very kind. She had two of the eldest girls under her charge, the children being confined to the nursery, with which she had no concern.

Charlotte, although remarking in a letter to her friend on the cleverness and sensibility with which Anne could express herself in epistolary correspondence, had some fear that, such was the natural diffidence of her manner, her mistress would sometimes believe her to have an impediment in her speech.

Charlotte's eagerness to obtain a situation was now so great that she does not seem to have considered well the step she was about to take, and she obtained one that was not satisfactory to her. It was in the family of a wealthy Yorkshire manufacturer; and we may well believe that the stylish surroundings of her employers differed materially from those of the family at Haworth. Here a large quantity of miscellaneous work was thrown on Charlotte, which displeased her and destroyed her comfort. In a letter to Emily, she says she is 'overwhelmed with oceans of needlework; yards of cambric to hem, muslin night-caps to make, etc.' She found the outside attractions of the house beautiful in 'pleasant woods, white paths, green lawns, and blue, sunshiny sky;' but these surroundings did not compensate for the humiliations which her situation imposed upon her, and her mistress and she did not like each other; so Charlotte did not return to the place after the July holidays of 1839.

Branwell was as yet unemployed, and he sought, and took much pleasure in the scenery, the events and circumstances of the hills and valleys of the West-Riding of Yorkshire, and was frequently from home. He went about the country, associating with the people, and revelling in their ready wit, which enabled him afterwards, by such observations and experience, to give vivid pictures of life and character. At the time of the Haworth 'Rushbearing,' of July, 1839, he visited Liverpool with one or two friends, and, while there, in compliance with an injunction of his father, made a stenographic report, at St. Jude's church, of a sermon by the Rev. H. McNeile, the well-known evangelical preacher. Here, a sudden attack of Tic compelled him to resort to opium, in some form, as an anodyne, whose soothing effect in pain he had previously known. Subsequently, passing a music shop, in one of their rambles through the town, Branwell's attention was arrested by a copy of the oratorio of 'Samson,' by Handel, displayed in the window, the performance of which had always excited him to the highest degree, and he eagerly besought his friend to purchase it, as well as some Mass, and various oratorio music, which was done.

On their return from Liverpool, Branwell, being under some

obligation to his friend, proffered to paint his portrait, to which Mr. M—— agreed. A sitting once a week was decided upon, to be in the room at the parsonage where Branwell studied and painted. On his visits, Mr. M—— invariably noticed a row of potatoes, placed on the uppermost rib of the range to roast, Branwell being very fond of them done in this way, even as Jane Eyre was in the novel. 'That night,' she says, 'on going to bed, I forgot to prepare, in imagination, the Barmecide supper of hot roast potatoes ... with which I was wont to amuse my inward cravings.' When Mr. M—— paid his weekly visits to the parsonage he always heard some one speaking aloud in the room adjoining Branwell's studio; and, at last, his curiosity being excited, he inquired whom it was. Branwell answered that it was his father committing his Sunday's sermon to memory. When the portrait was ready for the finishing touches, Mr. M—— discovered that Branwell had painted the names of Johann Sebastian Bach, Mozart, Haydn, and Handel at each corner of the canvas respectively. He remonstrated, but Branwell was firm, maintaining that, as his friend was an accomplished musician, and could perform the most elaborate and difficult compositions of these immortal men, with expression and ease, he was, in every way, worthy of being associated with them in the manner he designed. Mr. M—— complied. When the portrait was finished, Branwell pressed his friend to take a glass of wine; and, while the two were chatting over the affair, Mr. Brontë and his daughters entered the room to view Branwell's work on its completion. They were pleased with it, and praised it as a truthful likeness and an excellent picture.

We may well imagine the enthusiasm with which Branwell would recount his experience of Liverpool. How much he would have to tell of the wonders of the Mersey, the great ships that rode upon its surface, and its commerce with the new world, out across the ocean! His visit seems to have originated a proposal that the family should spend a week or a fortnight at that sea-port, but, almost at the same moment, Charlotte's friend suggested to her that they should visit Cleethorpes together, a suggestion that pleased her very much.

'The idea of seeing the sea,' she says, 'of being near it—watching its changes by sunrise, sunset, moonlight, and noon-day—in calm, perhaps in storm—fills and satisfies my mind. I shall be discontented at nothing. And then I am not to be with a set of people with whom I have nothing in common—who would be nuisances and bores.'

The visit of Charlotte to the sea-side seems to have been put off again and again, by often-recurring obstacles. The irresolution of her family in regard to the Liverpool project, and the manifest unwillingness that she should leave home on a visit anywhere else, put off, from time to time, the pleasure she had anticipated for herself; but at last she decided to go. Her box was packed and everything prepared, but no conveyance could be procured. Mr. Brontë objected to her going by coach, and walking part of the way to meet her friend, and her aunt exclaimed against 'the weather, and the roads, and the four winds of heaven,' so Charlotte almost gave up hope. She told her friend that the elders of the house had never cordially acquiesced in the measure, and that opposition was growing more open, though her father would willingly have indulged her. Even he, however, wished her to remain at home. Charlotte was 'provoked' that her aunt had deferred opposition until arrangements had been made. In the end 'E' was asked to pay a visit to the parsonage.

Owing to the circumstances indicated, Charlotte's visit to the sea-coast was put off until the following September, when an opportunity occurred favourable to the project, which does not seem to have been entirely abandoned; and she and her friend visited Easton where they spent a fortnight. Here for the first time Charlotte beheld the sea.

Afterwards she wrote, 'Have you forgotten the sea by this time, E.? Is it grown dim in your mind? Or can you still see it, dark, blue and green and foam-white, and hear it roaring roughly when the wind is high, or rushing softly when it is calm?' The Liverpool journey appears to have been finally abandoned.

It was in a letter, written about this time that Mrs. Gaskell found the first mention of a succession of curates who henceforth revolved round Haworth Parsonage. Three years earlier Mr. Brontë had sought aid from the 'Additional Curates' Society,' or some similar institution, and was provided at once with assistance. The increasing duties of his chapelry had rendered this step necessary. It would seem also that a curate was appointed to Stanbury, while another became master of the National or Grammar School. These gentlemen were not infrequent in their visits to the parsonage, and they varied the life of its inmates, sometimes one way and sometimes another. This circumstance, at the same time, provided Charlotte Brontë with those living studies which she did not fail afterwards to remember in her delineation of the three curates in 'Shirley.' Emily, on the other hand, invariably avoided these gentlemen.

The arrival of the curates at Haworth was the occasion of increased activity in the affairs of the chapelry; and, the church-rate question being uppermost at this juncture, the new-comers entered into a crusade against the Dissenters who had refused to pay church-rates. Charlotte wrote a long letter in which she spoke of a violent public meeting held at Haworth about the affair, and of two sermons against dissent—one by Mr. W. a 'noble, eloquent, high-church, apostolical-succession discourse, in which he banged the Dissenters most fearlessly and unflinchingly;' the other by Mr. C., a 'keener, cleverer, bolder, and more heart-stirring harangue,' than Charlotte, perhaps, had ever heard from the Haworth pulpit. She, however, did not entirely agree with either of these gentlemen, and thought, if she had been a Dissenter, she would have 'taken the first opportunity of kicking or of horse-whipping both.'

In the winter of 1839-40, Charlotte employed her leisure in the composition of a story which she had commenced on a scale commensurate with one of Richardson's novels of seven or eight volumes. Mrs. Gaskell saw some fragments of the manuscript, written in a very small hand: but she was less solicitous to decipher it, as Charlotte had herself condemned it in the preface to 'The Professor.' Branwell, to whom she submitted it, seems to have understood, at the time, that in its florid style of composition she was working in opposition to her genius, and he told her she was making a mistake. It appears not unlikely that Branwell was himself similarly engaged on prose writing when he gave her this opinion. A few months later, however, Charlotte resolved to send the commencement of her tale to Wordsworth, and that an unfavourable judgment was the result, for which she was not altogether unprepared, may be gathered from the following letter she addressed to the poet:—

'Authors are generally very tenacious of their productions, but I am not so much attached to this but that I can give it up without much distress. No doubt if I had gone on I should have made quite a Richardsonian concern of it.... I had materials in my head for half-a-dozen volumes.... Of course it is with considerable regret I relinquish any scheme so charming as the one I have sketched. It is very edifying and profitable to create a world out of your own brains, and people it with inhabitants who are so many Melchisedecs, and have no father or mother but your own imagination.... I am sorry I did not exist fifty or sixty years ago, when the "Ladies' Magazine" was flourishing like a green bay-tree. In that case, I make no doubt, my aspirations after literary fame would have met with due encouragement, and I should have had the pleasure of introducing Messrs. Percy and West into the best society, and recording all their sayings and doings in double-columned, close-printed pages.... I recollect, when I was a child, getting hold of some antiquated volumes, reading them by stealth with the most exquisite pleasure. You give a correct description of the patient Grisels of these days. My aunt was one of them, and to this day she thinks the tales of the "Ladies' Magazine" infinitely superior to any trash of modern literature. So do I; for I read them in childhood, and childhood has a very strong faculty of admiration, but a very weak one of criticism.... I am pleased that you cannot quite decide whether I am an attorney's clerk or a novel-reading dressmaker. I will not help you at all in the discovery....'

In the midst of their literary endeavours, their efforts were not relaxed to obtain new places. Charlotte was obliged by circumstances to give up her subscriptions to the Jews, and she determined to force herself to take a situation, if one could be found, though she says, 'I hate and abhor the very thoughts of governess-ship.' An alternative which the sisters talked over in these holidays was the opening of a school at Haworth, for which an enlargement of the parsonage would be required.

Branwell was more successful in his pursuit of employment than Charlotte, having procured the place of a tutor; and he was to commence his duties with the new year. Charlotte says of this event, 'One thing, however, will make the daily routine more unvaried than ever. Branwell, who used to enliven us, is to leave us in a few days, and enter the situation of a private tutor in the neighbourhood of Ulverston. How he will like to settle remains yet to be seen. At present he is full of hope and resolution. I, who know his variable nature, and his strong turn for active life, dare not be too sanguine.'

Branwell seems to have paid a farewell visit to the 'Lodge of the Three Graces' on the Christmas Day of this year, when he acted as organist. This is the only occasion on which he is recorded as having attended at the meetings of the Lodge in 1839, and it is the last on which his name appears in the minute book of the Haworth masonic body.

CHAPTER XVI.

BRANWELL AT BROUGHTON-IN-FURNESS.

The District of Black Comb—Branwell's Sonnet—and
Hartley Coleridge—'s Letter to the 'Old Knave of Trumps'—
Publication by Miss Robinson in her 'Emily Brontë'—'s
familiar Acquaintance with the People of Haworth—could
Paint their Characters with Accuracy—Knowledge of the
Human Passions—'s Isolation.

Branwell, being as desirous of employment as his sisters, had
sought for, and obtained, a situation as tutor in the family of Mr.
Postlethwaite, of Broughton-in-Furness. He entered upon his
new duties on the 1st of January, 1840.

Now that he found himself resident near the English lake
district, consecrated as it is by so many poetic memories, and dear
to him as the home of Wordsworth, Coleridge, and Southey he
naturally felt an intense interest in all that surrounded him; and,
when he was not engaged in teaching the sons of his employer,
he took occasion to visit such places as had any attraction for
him. On one of his pedestrian excursions, he had stepped into a
wayside inn, and was seated musing before the parlour fire, when
a young gentleman entered the room. Branwell turned round,
and recognized at once a friend of the name of Ayrton, whose
acquaintance he had formed in Leeds. The surprise and delight
at this unexpected meeting was mutual; and Branwell's friend,
who was driving about the country, requested his company for
some distance on the journey, for the purpose of prolonging
the interview, and of continuing the conversation that had been

begun. The young tutor drove some ten miles with his friend, utterly regardless of the long return walk to Ulverston.

Branwell delighted in the writings of the 'Lake Poets,' and was much influenced by Southey's prose works. He read the 'Life of Nelson,' and was himself moved to write a poem illustrative of the life of that great naval hero. He also read the 'Colloquies on Society,' and others of Southey's works. But it was Wordsworth who at this moment, was the object of Branwell's chief admiration. He revelled in that poet's fine description of the view from the top of Black Comb, and, perhaps, knew the lines written by his 'deity of the mind' on a stone on the side of the mountain, and probably had himself looked from its summit. But Branwell certainly knew Black Comb from afar. Five miles away he could see it; and he celebrated it in the following sonnet:

BLACK COMB.

'Far off, and half revealed, 'mid shade and light,
   Black Comb half smiles, half frowns; his mighty form
Scarce bending into peace—more formed to fight
   A thousand years of struggles with a storm
   Than bask one hour, subdued by sunshine warm,
To bright and breezeless rest; yet even his height
Towers not o'er this world's sympathies, he smiles—
While many a human heart to pleasures' wiles
   Can bear to bend, and still forget to rise—
As though he, huge and heath-clad, on our sight,
   Again rejoices in his stormy skies.
Man loses vigour in unstable joys.
Thus tempests find Black Comb invincible,
While we are lost, who should know life so well!'

It was doubtless while Branwell was living at Ulverston that he obtained the favourable opinion of Wordsworth on some poems which he submitted for criticism. Probably he found opportunity to visit the writer whose works he 'loved most in our literature,' and it would be on some similar excursion that he obtained an encouraging expression of opinion from Hartley Coleridge. The author of 'The Northern Worthies' was not unknown to the circle at 'The George,' at Bradford, and was acquainted with Branwell Brontë and Leyland.

The master of the 'Lodge of the Three Graces,' at Haworth, did not, however, long permit Branwell to forget his old acquaintance there; for this worthy soon addressed to him a communication which provoked a reply that Branwell dated from Broughton-in-Furness on the 13th of the March following his arrival. This unfortunate response, in which Branwell addressed the masonic sexton of Haworth, with sarcastic humour, as 'Old Knave of Trumps,' is the one which Miss Robinson has been so ill advised as to publish in her 'Emily Brontë;' and which has done not a little to draw down on the head of Branwell the full and unmitigated volume of Mr. Swinburne's vocabulary of abuse. And, in fact, if this letter could be taken as the proper and natural expression of an abject profligate, altogether shameless and unredeemed, he could find a defender neither here nor elsewhere. But there are good reasons for hoping that it was otherwise. We have seen that Branwell had been led to join the rude village society of Haworth, where, on account of his brilliance, and of his position as the incumbent's son, he was not a little looked up to. It was natural, then, that he should be led, foolishly enough, to endeavour to stand well with the friends he had selected, and his knowledge of character was sufficiently good to enable him to know what kind of letter would best suit the tastes and inclinations of many of his companions of the 'Lodge of the Three Graces.' He assumed in fact, that bravado of vice, that air of *diablerie*, which was thought by many people, in those days, and is so yet by not a few, to be the best proof of manhood, because it betokened a knowledge of the world. Yet, at the end of the letter,—the passage is not given by Miss Robinson—Branwell appears to take it as a matter of course that the sexton will not show it, and he begs him, for 'Heaven's sake,' to blot out the lines scored in red. Branwell knew the 'Old Knave of Trumps' well, and he was certain that his letter would cause no little amusement among his immediate friends to whom the sexton was sure to read it. He was ashamed of certain passages in it, which is evidence enough that it was not the outcome of a depraved and shameless nature, but rather the expression of the *acted* character of a vicious and *blasé* worldling. And it is, moreover, inconceivable that a young man, who was of the sensitive nature betokened by the contemporary poems we have published, could, at the same time, have been a hardened and cynical profligate. Indeed, it is evident that the objectionable allusions were not of his origination, but were called forth by the remarks of others, for whom Branwell does not fail to show his contempt.

It has, however, been the misfortune of Branwell Brontë, that a letter which he wrote in folly, for the eyes of personal friends alone, has been published to the world as the token and evidence of his infamy. One use, at any rate, flows from the publication of it, for it shows us the quick and vivid grasp of character, and the incisive mode of composition which now began, in his more vigorous moods, to distinguish its author. The letter is as follows:—

'BROUGHTON-IN-FURNESS,

'MARCH 13, 1840.

'Old Knave of Trumps,

'Don't think I have forgotten you, though I have delayed so long in writing to you. It was my purpose to send you a yarn as soon as I could find materials to spin one with, and it is only just now that I have had time to turn myself round and know where I am. If you saw me now, you would not know me, and you would laugh to hear the character the people give me. Oh, the falsehood and hypocrisy of this world! I am fixed in a little retired town by the sea-shore, among wild woody hills that rise round me—huge, rocky, and capped with clouds. My employer is a retired county magistrate, a large landowner, and of a right hearty and generous disposition. His wife is a quiet, silent, and amiable woman, and his sons are two fine, spirited lads. My landlord is a respectable surgeon, and six days out of seven is as drunk as a lord! His wife is a bustling, chattering, kind-hearted soul; and his daughter!—oh! death and damnation! Well, what am I? That is, what do they think I am? A most calm, sedate, sober, abstemious, patient, mild-hearted, virtuous, gentlemanly philosopher,—the picture of good works, and the treasure-house of righteous thoughts. Cards are shuffled under the table-cloth, glasses are thrust into the cupboard, if I enter the room. I take neither spirits, wine, nor malt liquors. I dress in black, and smile like a saint or martyr. Everybody says, "What a good young gentleman is Mr. Postlethwaite's tutor!" This is fact, as I am a living soul, and right comfortably do I laugh at them. I mean to continue in their good opinion. I took a half year's farewell of old friend whisky at Kendal on the night after I left. There was a party of gentlemen at the Royal Hotel, and I joined them. We ordered in supper and whisky-toddy as "hot as hell!" They thought I was a physician, and put me in the chair. I gave sundry toasts, that were washed down at the same time, till the room spun round and the candles danced in our eyes. One of the guests was a respectable old gentleman with powdered head, rosy cheeks, fat paunch, and ringed fingers. He gave "The Ladies," ... after which he brayed off with a speech; and in two minutes, in the middle of a grand sentence, he stopped, wiped his head, looked wildly round, stammered, coughed, stopped again, and called for his slippers. The waiter helped him to bed. Next a tall Irish squire and a native of the land of Israel began to quarrel about their countries; and, in the warmth of argument, discharged their glasses, each at his neighbour's throat instead of his own. I recommended bleeding, purging, and blistering; but they administered each other a real "Jem Warder," so I flung my tumbler on the floor, too, and swore I'd join "Old Ireland!" A regular rumpus ensued, but we were tamed at last. I found myself in bed next morning, with a bottle of porter, a glass, and a corkscrew beside me. Since then I have not tasted anything stronger than milk-and-water, nor, I hope, shall, till I return at Midsummer; when we will see about it. I am getting as fat as Prince William at Springhead, and as godly as his friend, Parson Winterbotham. My hand shakes no longer. I ride to the banker's at Ulverston with Mr. Postlethwaite, and sit drinking tea and talking scandal with old ladies. As to the young ones! I have one sitting by me just now—fair-faced, blue-eyed, dark-haired, sweet eighteen—she little thinks the devil is so near her!

'I was delighted to see thy note, old squire, but I do not understand one sentence—you will perhaps know what I mean…. How are all about you? I long to hear and see them again. How is the "Devil's Thumb," whom men call —— ——, and the "Devil in Mourning," whom they call —— ——? How are —— ——, and —— ——, and the Doctor; and him who will be used as the tongs of hell— he whose eyes Satan looks out of, as from windows—I mean —— ——, esquire? How are little —— ——, —— "Longshanks," —— ——, and the rest of them? Are they married, buried, devilled, and damned? When I come I'll give them a good squeeze of the hand; till then I am too godly for them to think of. That bow-legged devil used to ask me impertinent questions which I answered him in kind. Beelzebub will make of him a walking-stick! Keep to thy teetotalism, old squire, till I return; it will mend thy old body.... Does "Little Nosey" think I have forgotten him? No, by Jupiter! nor his clock either. [30] I'll send him a remembrancer some of these days! But I must talk to some one prettier than thee; so good-night, old boy, and

'BELIEVE ME THINE,

'THE PHILOSOPHER.

'Write directly. Of course you won't show this letter; and, for Heaven's sake, blot out all the lines scored with red ink.'

This letter, as I have intimated, was never intended for more than a moment's amusement, at most, to a small circle of acquaintances at Haworth, and was not to exist after having been read. But John Brown kept the letter, which I saw and copied. It is a curious circumstance, illustrating the hold which it obtained over the Haworth circle, that, though the original was lost so long since as 1874, the brother of the sexton knew it by heart, and could repeat it with considerable accuracy. In this way it has been several times written down. No allusion would have been made to the letter in the present work, if Miss Robinson—strange to say—had not thought it a fitting embellishment for her 'Emily Brontë.' If Branwell had known its fate at the moment he wrote it, it would never have reached the 'Worshipful Master of the Lodge of the Three Graces,' but would have been committed to the flames by his own hand; for, as we have seen, he was ashamed of some expressions scored in red, which he begged might be obliterated.

This letter, however, is valuable; inasmuch as it shows what Branwell, at this young period of his life, knew about human nature, and the depths to which it can descend. He had penetrated into the passions, feelings, and dispositions of his acquaintances by frequent intercourse, by keen perception, and by familiar conversation. He had heard them, noticed them, and could paint their characters with unerring precision and vivid colouring. He was acquainted with the ways of society, and the customs of domestic life. The world was to him a picture-gallery, and all living things in it were studies of the deepest interest. His knowledge of men and manners, of the hard, implacable, and selfish, and also of the soft, tender, and gentle natures of men and women, enabled him to cast their stories of sorrow and gladness faithfully and well.

At the time when he had attained manhood, when his intellects were reaching their full development, he had already been drawn into society, and indoctrinated into the mysteries of Haworth life; and had become acquainted with the excesses of men older and harder than himself. It cannot be wondered at that, if he had learned more than is usual in youth, he did not escape the temptations attendant on the peculiar knowledge he had acquired. But, while *he* was thus passing through the crooked ways and reckless deviations of the world, obtaining a large crop of experiences, good and bad, his *sisters* were, for the most part, at home, living like recluses, and, when away, were still in similar seclusion. Of Emily, Charlotte says, 'I am bound to avow that she had scarcely more practical knowledge of the peasantry amongst whom she lived, than a nun has of the country people who sometimes pass her convent gates. My sister's disposition was not naturally gregarious; circumstances favoured and fostered her tendency to seclusion; except to go to church or take a walk on the hills, she rarely crossed the threshold of home. Though her feeling for the people round her was benevolent, intercourse with them she never sought, nor, with very few exceptions, ever experienced. And yet she knew them, knew their ways, their language, their family histories; she could hear of them with interest, and talk of them *with* detail, minute, graphic, and accurate; but with them she rarely exchanged a word.' [31] But Branwell walked and held personal intercourse, as we have seen, with the people whom Emily shunned; and his personal knowledge, and his unquestionable genius combined, enabled him to grasp and appreciate, to dissect with penetrating skill, and to estimate and define the tendency of the strong and marked character of the people around him. It is, therefore, doubly unfortunate that, from Branwell, we have little remaining in the way of graphic description, and that the rich treasures of observation which he outpoured have, for the most part, left their impressions only in the memories of those who were privileged to hear him discourse.

CHAPTER XVII.

BRANWELL AT SOWERBY BRIDGE.
—CHARLOTTE'S EXERTIONS.

Branwell's Appointment at Ulverston ends—gets a Situation
on the Railroad at Sowerby Bridge—at Luddenden Foot—
Friends' Reminiscences of him—and Emily reading French
Novels—Charlotte obtains a Situation—about Anne—
Project of the Sisters—'s keen Desire to visit Brussels —
Letter to her Aunt Branwell.

If the performance of the responsible duties of his appointment
at Mr. Postlethwaite's, which ended, at his father's wish, in the
June of 1840, had been felt by Branwell as a banishment from
the cheerful company of his Haworth acquaintances, it had
been still greater from his artistic and literary friends in the
neighbourhood of Bradford and Halifax. Hence he sought, with
a perseverance amounting to anxiety, to obtain a post on the
Leeds and Manchester Railway,—to the opening of which he had
looked forward with concern—at some place in the valley of the
Calder, near Halifax; and he received the appointment of clerk
in charge, at the station at Sowerby Bridge. Charlotte says of
Branwell's determination: 'a distant relation of mine, one Patrick
Branwell, has set off to seek his fortune in the wild, wandering,
adventurous, romantic, knight-errant-like capacity of clerk on
the Leeds and Manchester Railroad.' [32] Branwell commenced
his new occupation at Sowerby Bridge on the 1st of October,
1840, just before the opening of the line from Hebden Bridge to
Normanton.

As has been already seen, an acquaintance had existed between Branwell and Leyland; but now that the former had become a resident in the immediate neighbourhood, after his visits to the artist's studio had been interrupted for six months, or more, by his stay at Broughton-in-Furness, a more frequent intercourse followed between the two. It was on a bright Sunday afternoon in the autumn of 1840, at the desire of my brother, the sculptor, that I accompanied him to the station at Sowerby Bridge to see Branwell. The young railway clerk was of gentleman-like appearance, and seemed to be qualified for a much better position than the one he had chosen. In stature he was a little below the middle height; not 'almost insignificantly small,' as Mr. Grundy states, nor had he 'a downcast look;' neither was he 'a plain specimen of humanity.' [33] He was slim and agile in figure, yet of well-formed outline. His complexion was clear and ruddy, and the expression of his face, at the time, lightsome and cheerful. His voice had a ringing sweetness, and the utterance and use of his English were perfect. Branwell appeared to be in excellent spirits, and showed none of those traces of intemperance with which some writers have unjustly credited him about this period of his life.

My brother had often spoken to me of Branwell's poetical abilities, his conversational powers, and the polish of his education; and, on a personal acquaintance, I found nothing to question in this estimate of his mental gifts, and of his literary attainments.

Branwell stayed at Sowerby Bridge some months, whence he was transferred, in 1841, to Luddenden Foot, a place about a mile further up the valley, where a station had been recently fixed. Mr. Grundy, who was an assistant-engineer on the line, became acquainted with Branwell at the latter place; and says of it, 'there was no village near at hand,' and that, 'had a position been chosen for this strange creature, for the express purpose of driving him several steps to the bad, this must have been it.' [34]

Mr. Grundy must have spoken from memory only. The ancient

village of Luddenden Foot, within two minutes' walk of the station, with its population employed in the mills and manufactories of the neighbourhood, together with its two old hostelries of the 'Red Lion,' and the 'Shuttle and Anchor,' was surely sufficient to banish all solitude and wildness from the neighbourhood of Branwell's sojourn. Yet the change was scarcely a desirable one, and doubtless helped to disgust Branwell with his employment. It is to be regretted that the respective occupations of Branwell and Mr. Grundy were of such a nature as to prevent a regular and continual intercourse, and that distance of time and place have so far dimmed Mr. Grundy's reminiscences of his friend, that, valuable though the letters he has wisely preserved are, many inaccuracies have entered into his recollections of him, and Mrs. Gaskell's exaggerated account has had undue weight in the picture he has drawn.

Mr. William Heaton, author of a minor volume of poems entitled the 'Flowers of Caldervale,' knew Branwell Brontë well when he was at Luddenden Foot. He wrote to me a letter in which occurred the following description of his mind and character, and also of his conversation when at one of the village inns, where they sometimes met:—

'He was,' says Heaton, 'blithe and gay, but at times appeared downcast and sad; yet, if the subject were some topic that he was acquainted with, or some author he loved, he would rise from his seat, and, in beautiful language, describe the author's character, with a zeal and fluency I had never heard equalled. His talents were of a very exalted kind. I have heard him quote pieces from the bard of Avon, from Shelley, Wordsworth, and Byron, as well as from Butler's "Hudibras," in such a manner as often made me wish I had been a scholar, as he was. At that time I was just beginning to write verses. It is true I had written many pieces, but they had never seen the light; and, on a certain occasion, I showed him one, which he pronounced very good. He lent me books which I had never seen before, and was ever ready to give me information. His temper was always mild towards me.

I shall never forget his love for the sublime and beautiful works of Nature, nor how he would tell of the lovely flowers and rare plants he had observed by the mountain stream and woodland rill. All these had excellencies for him; and I have often heard him dilate on the sweet strains of the nightingale, and on the thoughts that bewitched him the first time he heard one.'

During Branwell's twelvemonths' stay at Luddenden Foot, he formed new acquaintances, but the avocations, tastes, and pursuits of the well-to-do inhabitants did not accord with his; and he, perhaps, more frequently than was compatible with his duties, visited Halifax to seek the intellectual enjoyment which his own narrow occupation and the society of Luddenden Foot did not afford.

While he was occupied in the service of the railway company at this place, we hear nothing relating to him, of moment, in Charlotte's correspondence. Happy that he was employed, his sisters engaged eagerly and earnestly in devising schemes for obtaining a livelihood that might enable them to work together for their mutual assistance in literary labour.

Charlotte was still at home with Emily, reading French novels, of which, we learn, she had got another bale, 'containing upwards of forty volumes.' 'I have read about half,' she says. 'They are like the rest, clever, wicked, sophistical, and immoral. The best of it is, they give one a thorough idea of France and Paris, and are the best substitute for French conversation.' We scarcely recognize, in this employment, the Charlotte Brontë of three years before, whose religious mania was driving her to despair, unless, indeed, it be in the force with which she pursues the new bent of her inclination. She has read twenty volumes of this, the second, batch, and was proposing to read twenty more. It was her expectation that, by this process, she would become sufficiently familiar with the language to enable her to teach it to others.

In the letter in which she announced that Branwell had gone to his post on the railway—written in good spirits, when she saw everything *couleur-de-rose*, which, however, she attributes to the high wind blowing over the 'hills of Judea' at Haworth—she says: 'A woman of the name of Mrs. B——, it seems, wants a teacher. I wish she would have me; and I have written to Miss Wooler to tell her so. Verily, it is a delightful thing to live at home, at full liberty to do just what one pleases. But I recollect some scrubby old fable about grasshoppers and ants, by a scrubby old knave, yclept Æsop; the grasshoppers sang all the summer, and starved all the winter.'

Branwell was proving himself no grasshopper, for, if he sang, he was anxious to exert himself in a practical way at the same time; and, so far, he was doing well at Luddenden Foot. Charlotte, too, was resolved to be employed, but the negotiation with Mrs. B—— failed. The lady expressed herself pleased with the frankness with which Charlotte stated her qualifications, but she required some one who could undertake to give instruction in music and singing. This Miss Brontë could not do. She does not appear to have had the musical taste which her brother and sisters had inherited from the Branwell family. She resembled her father, perhaps, more closely than did any of the other children. At last, however, in March, 1841, she entered her second situation as a private governess. 'I told you, some time since,' she writes to her friend, 'that I meant to get a situation, and, when I said so, my resolution was quite fixed. I felt that, however often I was disappointed, I had no intention of relinquishing my efforts. After being severely baffled two or three times—after a world of trouble, in the way of correspondence and interviews—I have at length succeeded, and am fairly established in my new place.'

Charlotte found her residence not very large, but the grounds were fine and extensive. She had made some sacrifice to secure comfort, as she says, not good living, but cheerful faces and warm hearts. Her pupils were two in number, one a girl of eight, and the other a boy of six. Though always more or less afflicted with home-sickness, whenever she was at a distance from her father's house, with its familiar and affectionate ways, she enjoyed, in her new place, considerable relief from it, owing to the spontaneous generosity and kindliness of her employers. She says, indeed, 'My earnest wish and endeavour will be to please them. If I can but feel that I am giving satisfaction, and if, at the same time, I can keep my health, I shall, I hope, be moderately happy. But no one but myself can tell how hard a governess's work is to me—for no one but myself is aware how utterly averse my whole mind and nature are for the employment. Do not think that I fail to blame myself for this, or that I leave any means unemployed to conquer this feeling. Some of my greatest difficulties lie in things that would appear to you comparatively trivial. I find it so hard to repel the rude familiarity of children. I find it so difficult to ask either servants or mistress for anything I want, however much I want it. It is less pain for me to endure the greatest inconvenience than to go into the kitchen to request its removal. I am a fool. Heaven knows I cannot help it.'

Charlotte found matters a little easier after the first month of her stay, and her home-sickness became less oppressive. Though her time was much occupied, great kindness was shown towards her, and her father and her friend were invited to come to see her.

In June she wrote, in the absence of her employer, 'You can hardly fancy it possible, I dare say, that I cannot find a quarter-of-an-hour to scribble a note in; but so it is; and when a note is written, it has to be carried a mile to the post, and that consumes nearly an hour, which is a large portion of the day. Mr. and Mrs. —— have been gone a week. I heard from them this morning. No time is fixed for their return, but I hope it will not be delayed long, or I shall miss the chance of seeing Anne this vacation. She came home, I understand, last Wednesday, and is only to be allowed three weeks' vacation, because the family she is with are going to Scarborough. *I should like to see her,* to judge for myself of the state of her health. I dare not trust any other person's report, no one seems minute enough in their observations. I should very much have liked you to have seen her. I have got on very well with the servants and children so far; yet it is dreary, solitary work. You can tell as well as me the lonely feeling of being without a companion.' [35]

The delicate Anne, struggling with all the troubles, the indignities, of the life of a governess, was a picture that was naturally distressing enough to Charlotte, ever anxious, ever watchful over the welfare of her youngest sister, and she would, perhaps, be apt, in her imagination, to exaggerate her sister's difficulties in the light of her own. In truth the sisters had qualities of mind and heart which did much to unfit them for the enjoyment of content or happiness amongst strangers. Charlotte, in particular, with a nature, sensitive, observant, and tenacious; an imagination highly wrought, active, and fertile, but too often morbid; with a will, powerful, yet constrained by the nervous weakness of an excitable constitution, could with difficulty conform inclination to the necessities of such a career; she longed for freedom. It was not surprising, then, that when Charlotte reached Haworth—which she did before Anne's return—there was a revival of the project I have before mentioned of the opening of a school, wherein they could enjoy the liberty of home.

Mr. Brontë and Miss Branwell were not unfavourably disposed towards the project, and they conversed now and then, at the breakfast-table or in the evenings, as to how they could best help the girls into the position they so much coveted. The sisters must always have had a friend in their father in these matters; he could not but be pleased and interested in struggles and expectations which reproduced so closely the hopeful days of his own early life, and we learn, as the result of the deliberations of the elders, that the aunt offered a loan, or intimated that she would, perhaps, offer one, in case her nieces could give some assurance of the solidity of their plans in the shape of a situation decided upon and of pupils promised. The East-Riding was thought to be not so well provided with schools as the West, and the favourite idea of the sisters was to open their projected academy in the neighbourhood of Burlington, where the health, both of themselves and of their pupils, might be hoped for. But there was a question how much their aunt would be disposed to advance them. Charlotte did not think she would sink more than £150 in such a venture, and she doubted if this would be a sufficient sum with which to establish a school and commence house-keeping, on however modest a scale. These were reflections which damped a little the excitement of hopeful expectation in which the sisters, especially Charlotte, revolved these plans. She anxiously awaited the coming of her friend, on the day she was expected to visit them during their holidays at the parsonage, wearying her eyes with watching from the window, eye-glass in hand, and, sometimes, spectacles on nose, eager to talk over her schemes with some one else than her sisters and to hear a new opinion. But her friend could not come, and she says, 'a hundred things I had to say to you will now be forgotten, and never said.' Charlotte began to fear some time must elapse before her plans could be executed, and she resolved not to relinquish her situation till something was assured. But this expectation of keeping a school, cherished through long years, was never realized by the sisters; ever and anon the shifting sands of circumstance, the changing currents of life, moved them away, even while they believed themselves approaching the goal of their hopes.

Charlotte returned to her situation, and she tells her friend, in a letter dated August the 7th, 1841, that she 'felt herself' again. Mr. and Mrs. —— were from home, and she takes the opportunity of saying that to be solitary there was to her the happiest part of her time. She enters into particulars of the household: the children were under decent control, and the servants were observant and attentive to her; she says of herself, moreover, that the absence of the master and mistress relieved her from the duty of always putting on the appearance of being cheerful and conversable.

Her friends, Martha and Mary T——, were enjoying great advantages on the Continent, where they had gone to stay a month with their brother. Charlotte had had a long letter from Mary, and a packet enclosing a handsome black silk scarf, and a pair of beautiful kid gloves bought in Brussels as a present. She was pleased with them, and that she had been remembered so far off, amidst the excitement of 'one of the most splendid capitals of Europe.' Mary's letters spoke of 'some of the pictures and cathedrals she had seen—pictures the most exquisite, cathedrals the most venerable.' Something swelled to the throat of Charlotte as she read this account. She was seized with a 'vehement impatience of restraint and steady work; such a strong wish for wings—wings such as wealth can furnish; such an urgent thirst to see, to know, to learn; something internal seemed to expand bodily for a minute.' She was tantalized for a time by the consciousness of faculties unexercised; then all collapsed. She considered these emotions, momentary as they were, rebellious and absurd, and they were speedily quelled by the resolute spirit they had disturbed. She hoped they would not revive, as they had been acutely painful. The school project, instead of at all fading, was gaining strength, and the three sisters kept it in view as the pole-star round which all their other schemes, as of lesser importance, revolved. To this they looked in their despondency. Charlotte was haunted, sometimes, and dismayed, at the conviction that she had no natural knack for her occupation. She says that, if teaching only were requisite, all would be smooth and easy; and she adds, 'but it is the living in other people's houses—the estrangement from one's real character—the adoption of a cold, rigid, apathetic exterior, that is painful.'

It appears that Miss Wooler was about this time intending to give up her school at Dewsbury Moor, and had offered it to the Misses Brontë. One or two disadvantages had to be set against the favourable terms on which they might have the school. The situation could not commend itself to Charlotte, anxious as she was concerning Anne's health; the number of pupils had also diminished, and it would be necessary to offer special advantages in the way of education before they could hope to have a prosperous establishment—so their friends argued. But Charlotte had resolved to take the school. The sisters, however, could not feel confident that their qualifications were such as would render success certain. Hence, a suggestion that was made to Charlotte which would provide her with the necessary powers, was at once taken up with all the energy of her nature; she thus writes to her aunt, on whom all must depend:

'SEPTEMBER 29TH, 1841.

'Dear Aunt,

'I have heard nothing of Miss Wooler yet since I wrote to her, intimating that I would accept her offer. I cannot conjecture the reason of this long silence, unless some unforeseen impediment has occurred in concluding the bargain. Meantime a plan has been suggested and approved by Mr. and Mrs. ——' (the father and mother of her pupils) 'and others, which I wish now to impart to you. My friends recommend me, if I desire to secure permanent success, to delay commencing the school for six months longer, and by all means to contrive, by hook or by crook, to spend the intervening time in some school on the continent. They say schools in England are so numerous, competition so great, that without some such step towards attaining superiority, we shall probably have a very hard struggle, and may fail in the end. They say, moreover, that the loan of £100, which you have been so kind as to offer us, will, perhaps, not be all required now, as Miss Wooler will lend us the furniture; and that, if the speculation is intended to be a good and successful one, half the sum, at least, ought to be laid out in the manner I have mentioned, thereby insuring a more speedy repayment both of interest and principal.

'I would not go to France or to Paris. I would go to Brussels in Belgium. The cost of the journey there, at the dearest rate of travelling, would be £5; living there is little more than half as dear as it is in England, and the facilities for education are equal or superior to any other place in Europe. In half a year, I could acquire a thorough familiarity with French. I could improve greatly in Italian, and even get a dash of German; *i.e.*, provided my health continued as good as it is now. Mary is now staying at Brussels, at a first-rate establishment there. I should not think of going to the Château de Kokleberg, where she is resident, as the terms are much too high; but if I wrote to her, she, with the assistance of Mrs. Jenkins, the wife of the British Chaplain, would be able to secure me a cheap, decent residence and respectable protection. I should have the opportunity of seeing her frequently; she would make me acquainted with the city; and, with the assistance of her cousins, I should probably be introduced to connections far more improving, polished, and cultivated, than any I have yet known.

'These are advantages which would turn to real account, when we actually commenced a school; and, if Emily could share them with me, we could take a footing in the world afterwards which we can never do now. I say Emily instead of Anne; for Anne might take her turn at some future period, if our school answered. I feel certain, while I am writing, that you will see the propriety of what I say. You always like to use your money to the best advantage. You are not fond of making shabby purchases; when you do confer a favour, it is often done in style; and depend upon it, £50 or £100, thus laid out, would be well employed. Of course I know no other friend in the world to whom I could apply on this subject except yourself. I feel an absolute conviction that, if this advantage were allowed us, it would be the making of us for life. Papa will, perhaps, think it a wild and ambitious scheme; but whoever rose in the world without ambition? When he left Ireland to go to Cambridge University, he was as ambitious as I am

now. I want us all to get on. I know we have talents, and I
want them to be turned to account. I look to you, aunt, to
help us. I think you will not refuse. I know, if you consent,
it shall not be my fault if you ever repent your kindness.'

Charlotte had some time to wait for an answer, but it came
at last; her enthusiasm had carried the day. The answer was
favourable: she and Emily were to go to Brussels.

At times, during his stay with the railway company, Branwell
would drive over from Luddenden Foot to visit his family at
the Haworth parsonage, having hired a gig for the purpose.
Mr. Grundy sometimes accompanied him, and they would
escape to the moors together, or pay curious visits to the old
fortune-teller, with the curates. Then, says his friend, he was
'at his best, and would be eloquent and amusing, though, on
returning sometimes, he would burst into tears, and swear he
meant to mend.' This last statement is favourable to Branwell's
calm judgment upon himself. Few—and Branwell was one
of the last—drift deliberately into wrong-doing. He was, like
most other men, often placed under influences which a habit of
attention and self-control would have enabled him to resist. He
knew, perhaps, in a desultory way, what he ought to do, and what
he ought not; but, owing to his inattention to consequences, he
might, now and then, go wrong, sometimes yielding to whatever
illusion was paramount within, acting in concert with whatever
was most alluring without; yet he could draw his mental forces
together, and review his past actions with keen and painful
accuracy. Hence he was not destitute of the faculty of analyzing
his acts in the light of their moral quality, and, when his sober
judgment enabled him to see them in their true bearing, he
exhibited a due contrition.

On Branwell's visits home, he learned much of the exertions,
the projects, and the resolves of his sisters. He was aware of their
aims, and how important were the steps being taken to qualify
them the better for teaching others, more especially in perfecting

their knowledge of the French language and of music. He also knew of the ultimate hope of his sisters—that, were the future secure, they would have leisure to realize their early dream of one day becoming authors, never relinquished, even when distance divided, and when absorbing tasks occupied them. He had the highest appreciation of their genius; and, although he had his times of hilarity, indulgence, and enjoyment, he was certainly never forgetful of his own hopes and aspirations in the same direction.

CHAPTER XVIII.

BRANWELL'S POETRY, 1842.

Situation of Luddenden Foot—Branwell visits Manchester—
Sultry Summer—visits the Picturesque Places adjacent—
impromptu Verses to Mr. Grundy—leaves the Railway
Company—Miss Robinson's unjust Comments—three
Sonnets—poem 'The Afghan War'—Branwell's letter to Mr.
Grundy—Self-depreciation.

Luddenden Foot—the second place of Branwell Brontë's
appointment as clerk in charge on the Leeds and Manchester
Railway—was a village about equi-distant between Sowerby
Bridge and Mytholmroyd, situated in a fertile and moderately-
wooded valley, on the left bank of the Calder as it descends
from its source in Cliviger Dean. The cultivated hills rise to a
considerable height on both sides of the river, and are very
romantic in character. Among the manufacturers and gentry
of the neighbourhood, Branwell found few to welcome him,
and from these he turned to the artists and literary men he had
previously known at Halifax.

But Branwell, in addition, made excursions up the valley (Mr.
W——, his fellow-assistant, acting for him in his absence) in the
direction of Hebden Bridge, Heptonstall, the Ridge, Todmorden,
and the heights of Wadsworth. There were, indeed, many places
of marvellous beauty and interest near, that have long been the
theme of artists and poets, with which he did not fail to make
himself acquainted.

The huge, rounded hills, which border this valley, are

intersected in places by lovely cloughs and glens, whose peat-stained streams rush over their rocky beds, from the elevated grouse-moors around, to pour their waters into the Calder. From Luddenden Dean, between the townships of Warley and Midgley, a brook makes its way to Luddenden Foot, through a glen on whose verdant slopes stand several ancient houses of architectural and historic interest. Among these are Ewood Hall, where Bishop Farrer was born, and Kershaw House, a beautiful Jacobean mansion. Crag Valley, which descends to the Calder on the opposite bank, a mile or more from Luddenden Foot, is deeper and more thickly wooded. On one hand lies Sowerby—with Haugh End, the birthplace of Archbishop Tillotson—and, on the other, Erringden, which was a royal deer-park in the days of the Plantagenets. But the loveliest of the valleys through which the confluent streams of the Calder run, is that of Hebden, a romantic glen, winding between the wooded and precipitous slopes of Heptonstall—crowned with the ancient and now ruined church of St. Thomas à Becket—and of Wadsworth, with its narrow dell of Crimsworth, which gave Charlotte Brontë a name for the hero of the earliest of her novels. Between these solemn heights the stream flows beneath the huge crags of Hardcastle, and roars over many a rocky obstruction in its channel before it reaches the Calder at Hebden Bridge. This was a district to which picnic-parties from Haworth often came, there being a direct road over the hills.

Branwell also visited Manchester on one occasion; and, on his return, he gave an account to a young clergyman, then living in the neighbourhood of Mytholmroyd, who sometimes went to his wooden shanty at Luddenden Foot to hear his conversation, of how he had been impressed with the architecture of the parish church at Manchester, as he stood under the arched portal, and beheld the long lines of pillars and arches, and the fretted roof, the lightsome details of which had charmed him. He went forward on that occasion to the choir of the church, and saw the Lady Chapel—which still retained its beautiful screen, with its Perpendicular tracery and shafts of that period—occupied by the gravedigger's implements, which reminded him of the 'Worshipful Master of the Lodge of the Three Graces,' consisting of crowbar, mattock, spade, barrow, planks and ropes; for the Lady Chapel had been made a convenient receptacle for these dismal chattels.

The summer of 1841 was a somewhat monotonous time for Branwell and his friend at the quiet station. Here, in the intervals of the trains, scarcely anything was heard except the occasional hum of a bee or a wasp, or the drone of a blue-bottle, while the almost vertical rays of a summer sun darted down on the roof of the wooden hut, and made the place unendurable. It was in moments of weary lassitude, or in hours of drowsy leisure, that Branwell whiled away the time by sketching carelessly on the margins of the books—for the amusement of himself and his friend—free-hand portraits of characters of the neighbourhood, and of the celebrated pugilists of the day.

But about Hebden Bridge there were people known to Branwell, and he did not fail to visit them. His sister, Charlotte, in after-years, sometimes came to Hanging Royd, Hebden Bridge, the house of my late friend, the Rev. Sutcliffe Sowden, then incumbent of Mytholm—the gentleman who afterwards performed the marriage ceremony between the gifted lady and Mr. Nicholls. The friendship of the latter and Mr. Sowden dated from earlier years, and to them Branwell was known when he was at Luddenden Foot. He had, indeed, sometimes clerical visitors at his 'wooden shanty' to hear his conversation. Mr. Sowden was an enthusiastic lover of scenery, and the sphere of his duties abounded in moors, wilds, crags, rivers, brooks, and dells, which he often visited. Branwell's tastes accorded with his, but these attractions clearly drew Branwell's attention, too often and too far, from the imperative duties of his situation, comparatively light though they were. As might be expected, therefore, the work of this talented but changeful young man was found unsatisfactory, and explanations were demanded. About the time of the close of his twelve months' official duties at Luddenden Foot, an examination of his books was made, and they were found to be confused and incomplete. The irregularity and the defects of his returns had also been remarked, and an inquiry was set on foot respecting them. The officials, in looking over the books, discovered the pen-and-ink sketches on the margins of the pages, which I have already mentioned; and these were taken as conclusive evidence of carelessness and indifference on the part of the unfortunate Branwell in the performance of his duties and the keeping of his accounts.

He had been made aware, by unwelcome inquiries and remonstrances, that his position with the railway company was precarious, and he was filled with apprehension as to the ultimate consequences. He was requested finally to appear at the audit of the company, and his friend W—— accompanied him.

It was at the Christmas of 1841, that the Brontës expected to meet at home together, in anticipation of Charlotte and Emily's journey to Brussels; but Charlotte had not found her brother there in the January of 1842, for she writes on the 20th of that month and year: 'I have been every week, since I came home, expecting to see Branwell, and he has never been able to get over yet. We fully expect him, however, next Saturday.' [36] Branwell certainly returned home, but only when it had been intimated to him that his services were no longer required by the railway company. How far he had felt the duties of his post irksome, and the power of perseverance required inconsistent with his tastes and pursuits, does not appear, though the inference that they were so will scarcely be doubted. But the humiliation and sorrow he felt on the loss of his employment plunged him, for a time, into despair; and the natural gloom of his disposition, caused him to magnify the common pleasures and enjoyments of his leisure hours into crimes and omissions of duty of no ordinary magnitude. But the erroneous recollections of Mr. Grundy, respecting the situation of the station at Luddenden Foot, and its supposed deleterious influence on Branwell's manners and obligations, may justify a doubt as to the particular accuracy of many of his reminiscences of his friend.

The following incident of Branwell's stay at that place, which Mr. Grundy gives, may be regarded as affording a valuable contribution to his writings; for, although impromptu, the verses show that he could, even on unexpected occasions, bring into play his innate faculty of verse with no mean grasp of his subject, and a certain harmony of rhythmical expression.

Mr. Grundy says, 'On one occasion he (Branwell) thought I was disposed to treat him distantly at a party, and he retired in great dudgeon. When I arrived at my lodgings the same evening, I found the following, necessarily an impromptu:—

'"The man who will not know another,
    Whose heart can never sympathize,
Who loves not comrade, friend, or brother,
    Unhonoured lives—unnoticed dies:
His frozen eye, his bloodless heart,
Nature, repugnant, bids depart.

'"O, Grundy! born for nobler aim,
Be thine the task to shun such shame;
And henceforth never think that he
Who gives his hand in courtesy
To one who kindly feels to him,
His gentle birth or name can dim.

'"However mean a man may be,
Know man *is* man as well as thee;
However high thy gentle line,
Know he who writes can rank with thine;
And though his frame be worn and dead,
Some light still glitters round his head.

'"Yes! though his tottering limbs seem old,

179

His heart and blood are not yet cold.
Ah, Grundy! shun his evil ways,
His restless nights, his troubled days;
But never slight his mind, which flies,
Instinct with noble sympathies,
Afar from spleen and treachery,
To thought, to kindness, and to thee.

"'P. B. Brontë.'" [37]

Branwell's extreme sensibility caused him, indeed, to exaggerate both the lights and the shadows of his existence. He was gleeful, as I found, full of fun, jest, and anecdote, in social circles, or where literature and art were the theme; and then, almost involuntarily, would rise to his feet, and, with a beaming countenance, treat the subject with a vivid flow of imagination, displaying the rich stores of his information with wondrous and enthralling eloquence. But, under disappointment or misfortune, he fell a prey to gloomy thoughts, and reached a state often near akin to despair. It was at such moments that he usually took up his pen to express, in poetry, the fulness of his feelings and the depth of his sorrow; and it is to this fact that the pathetic sadness of most of his writings is due. I have had occasion already to speak of the melancholy tone which characterized also the minds of his sisters.

The worth of Branwell's poetic genius about this time,—the year of 1842,—has been unfairly commented upon. Miss Robinson, questioning the judgment of the Brontë sisters, undertakes to doubt if Branwell's mental gifts were any better than his moral qualities, and says: 'It is doubtful, judging from Branwell's letters and his verses, whether anything much better than his father's "Cottage in the Wood" would have resulted from his following the advice of James Montgomery. Fluent ease, often on the verge of twaddle, with here and there a bright felicitous touch, with here and there a smack of the conventional hymn-book and pulpit twang—such weak and characterless effusions are all that is left of the passion-ridden pseudo-genius of Haworth.' [38]

Miss Robinson's ignorance of Branwell's more matured poems and writings has caused her, in company with others, to fall into very grave errors regarding him; and she,—with extreme bitterness, it must be said,—has embellished her biography of Emily with elaborate censures of his misdeeds, and with accounts of his imputed glaring inferiority to his sisters in intellectual power. It is pitiable, indeed, that Miss Robinson,—and not she alone,—in the want of Branwell's true life and remains, with nothing to set against the primary errors of Mrs. Gaskell,—should have joined the hue and cry against him, and have essayed, almost as of set purpose, to write down the gifted brother of the author whose life she was giving to the world.

In 1842 Branwell began to feel more perceptibly the development of his intellectual powers, and to discern more clearly his natural ability to define, in poetic and felicitous language, his thoughts, feelings, and emotions. While under the depression and gloom consequent upon his disgrace, and the recent loss of his employment, he wrote the three following sonnets. The profound depth of feeling, expressed with mournful voice, which pervades them, the full consciousness of woe by which they are informed, leave nothing wanting in their expression of pathetic beauty; and they are distinguished by much sweetness of diction. These sonnets favourably show the poetical genius of Branwell. His soul is carried beyond his frail mortality; but sadness and sorrow, enshrouding his imagination, bind it to the precincts of the tomb. Here, with pessimistic and gloomy philosophy, he bids us, impressed with the slender sum of human happiness, to recognize the constant recurrence of the misery to which we are born, and to discern how little there is beneficent in nature or mankind.

SONNET I.

ON LANDSEER'S PAINTING.

'The Shepherd's Chief Mourner'—A Dog Keeping Watch at Twilight over its Master's Grave.

The beams of Fame dry up affection's tears;
   And those who rise forget from whom they spring;
   Wealth's golden glories—pleasure's glittering wing—
All that we follow through our chase of years—
All that our hope seeks—all our caution fears,
   Dim or destroy those holy thoughts which cling
   Round where the forms we loved lie slumbering;
But, not with *thee*—our slave—whose joys and cares
   We deem so grovelling—power nor pride are thine,
Nor our pursuits, nor ties; yet, o'er this grave,
Where lately crowds the form of mourning gave,
   I only hear *thy* low heart-broken whine—
   I only see *thee* left long hours to pine
For *him* whom thou—if love had power—would'st save!

SONNET II.

ON THE CALLOUSNESS PRODUCED BY CARE.

Why hold young eyes the fullest fount of tears?
   And why do youthful hearts the oftenest sigh,
   When fancied friends forsake, or lovers fly,
Or fancied woes and dangers wake their fears?
Ah! he who asks has known but spring-tide years,

Or Time's rough voice had long since told him why!
Increase of days increases misery;
And misery brings selfishness, which sears
The heart's first feelings: 'mid the battle's roar,
In Death's dread grasp, the soldier's eyes are blind
To comrades dying, and he whose hopes are o'er
Turns coldest from the sufferings of mankind;
A bleeding spirit oft delights in gore:
A tortured heart oft makes a tyrant mind.

SONNET III.

On Peaceful Death and Painful Life.

Why dost thou sorrow for the happy dead?
For, if their life be lost, their toils are o'er,
And woe and want can trouble them no more;
Nor ever slept they in an earthly bed
So sound as now they sleep, while dreamless laid
In the dark chambers of the unknown shore,
Where Night and Silence guard each sealed door.
So, turn from such as these thy drooping head,
And mourn the *Dead Alive*—whose spirit flies—
Whose life departs, before his death has come;
Who knows no Heaven beneath Life's gloomy skies,
Who sees no Hope to brighten up that gloom,—
'Tis *He* who feels the worm that never dies,—
The *real* death and darkness of the tomb.

It is painful to find the writer of these sad and beautiful sonnets spoken of in terms of reprobation, as being, at the time he wrote them, and when asking Mr. Grundy's aid while seeking a situation, 'sunk and contemptible.'

'Alas,' says Miss Robinson, 'no helping hand rescued the sinking wretch from the quicksands of idle sensuality which slowly engulfed him!' [39] Let us look further.

The Afghan War, which commenced in 1838, and had secured for the English arms what seemed at the time a complete conquest, was followed by the conspiracy of Akbar Khan, the son of Dost Mohammed, which occurred at the beginning of winter, when help from India was hopeless. There was an uprising at Cabul, and several officers and men were slain, which compelled Major Pottinger to submit to humiliating conditions. The British left Cabul; and the disastrous retreat to India, through the Khyber Pass, which commenced on January 6th, 1842, will long be sadly remembered. Of sixteen thousand troops—accompanied by women and children to the number of ten thousand more— who were continually harassed by hostile tribes on the way, and benumbed by the severity of the winter, only one man, Doctor Brydon, survived to tell the tidings. Branwell, overwhelmed by these horrors, published the following powerful and impressive poem in the 'Leeds Intelligencer,' on May the 7th of the same year.

THE AFGHAN WAR.

'Winds within our chimney thunder,
    Rain-showers shake each window-pane,
Still—if nought our household sunder—
    We can smile at wind or rain.
Sickness shades a loved one's chamber,
    Steps glide gently to and fro,
Still—'mid woe—our hearts remember
    We are there to soothe that woe.

'Comes at last the hour of mourning,
    Solemn tolls the funeral bell;
And we feel that no returning
    Fate allows to such farewell:
Still a holy hope shines o'er us;
    We wept by the One who died;
And 'neath earth shall death restore us;
    As round hearthstone—side by side.

'But—when all at eve, together,
    Circle round the flickering light,
While December's howling weather
    Ushers in a stormy night:
When each ear, scarce conscious, listens
    To the outside Winter's war,
When each trembling eyelash glistens
    As each thinks of *one* afar—

Man to chilly silence dying,
    Ceases story, song, and smile;
Thought asks—"Is the loved one lying
    Cold upon some storm-beat isle?"
And with death—when doubtings vanish,
    When despair still hopes and fears—
Though our anguish toil may banish,
    Rest brings unavailing tears.

'So, Old England—when the warning
    Of thy funeral bells I hear—
Though thy dead a host is mourning,
    Friends and kindred watch each bier.
But alas! Atlantic waters
    Bear another sound from far!
Unknown woes, uncounted slaughters,
    Cruel deaths, inglorious war!

'Breasts and banners, crushed and gory,
    That seemed once invincible;
England's children—England's glory,
    Moslem sabres smite and quell!
Far away their bones are wasting,
    But I hear their spirits call—
"Is our Mighty Mother hasting
    To avenge her children's fall?"

'England rise! Thine ancient thunder
    Humbled mightier foes than these;
Broke a whole world's bonds asunder,
    Gave thee empire o'er the seas:
And while yet one rose may blossom,
    Emblem of thy former bloom,
Let not age invade thy bosom—
    Brightest shine in darkest gloom!

'While one oak thy homes shall shadow,
    Stand like it as thou hast stood;
While a Spring greets grove and meadow,
    Let not Winter freeze thy blood.
Till this hour St. George's standard
    Led the advancing march of time;
England! keep it streaming vanward,
    Conqueror over age and clime!'

In this poem Branwell prefaces his subject with a picture of domestic suffering—one with which he is familiar—and compares the consolation which accompanies the affectionate attentions of those present, with the hopeless fate and untended deaths of such as perish in the storms and wars of distant places, far away from their homes and friends. In the true, loyal, and national spirit which animates him, his manly appeal to England, comprised principally in the last two verses, is perhaps one of the noblest and most vigorous ever written.

In the May of 1842, Leyland was commissioned to execute certain monuments for Haworth and its neighbourhood; and, on the 15th of that month, Branwell wrote to him, in reference to a design for a monument which he had sent for submission to a committee of which the Rev. P. Brontë was chairman, and invited him to the parsonage on the 20th of the month, being sure his father would be pleased to see him. Leyland visited Haworth and partook of Mr. Brontë's hospitality; and in the evening, accompanied by the incumbent and his son, appeared before the monument committee.

Branwell also wrote an interesting letter to Mr. Grundy on May 22nd, 1842, which that gentleman erroneously assigns to 1845. [40] In it he says that he cannot avoid the temptation, while sitting alone, all the household being at church, and he being the sole occupant of the parsonage, to scribble a few lines to cheer his spirits. He alludes to the extreme pain, illness, and mental depression he has endured since his dismissal. He describes himself, while at Luddenden Foot, as a 'miserable wreck,' as requiring six glasses of whisky to stimulate him, as almost insane! And he feels his recovery from this last stage of his condition to be retarded by 'having nothing to listen to except the wind moaning among old chimneys and older ash trees,—nothing to look at except heathery hills, walked over when life had all to hope for, and nothing to regret.' He reproaches himself, in bitter terms, with seeking indulgence, while at Luddenden Foot, in failings which formed, he declares, the black spot on his character. His sister Charlotte's mind appears to have been cast in the same gloomy mould; for, when suffering under bodily ailment, or the despondency and hopelessness which overshadowed her soul, she was impelled, as we have seen, to make confessions to her friend 'E' of her 'stings of conscience,' her 'visitings of remorse.' She hates her 'former flippancy and forwardness.' She is in a state of 'horrid, gloomy uncertainty,' and clouds are 'gathering darker,' and a more depressing despondency weighs upon her spirits. [41]

In another letter to her friend, Charlotte says she is 'in a strange state of mind—still gloomy, but not despairing. I keep trying to do right…. I abhor myself, I despise myself.' And again, later, she wonders if the new year will be 'stained as darkly as the last with all our sins, follies, secret vanities, and uncontrolled passions and propensities,' saying 'I trust not; but I feel in nothing better, neither humbler nor purer.' [42]

Branwell, however, while making, in a like tone, his unnecessarily exaggerated confession to his friend, sets forth his renovation of soul and body. He has, at length, acquired health, strength, and soundness of mind far superior to anything he had known at Luddenden Foot. He can speak cheerfully, and enjoy the company of another, without his former stimulus. He can write, think, and act, with some apparent approach to resolution, and he only wants a motive for exertion to be happier than he has been for years. He has still something left in him which might do him service. He thinks he ought not to live too long in solitude, as the world soon forgets those who wish it 'Goodbye.' Then, although ashamed of it, he asks for answers to some inquiries he had made about obtaining a new situation, evidently thinking Mr. Grundy's influence of importance in the matter.

This letter must receive a passing notice. It shows Branwell's mind vigorous and healthy, although it had been disordered by physical illness accompanied by brooding melancholy. His picture of the lonely parsonage and the solitude of the surrounding country, combined with the expression of his own sad emotions, is graphic enough. His sisters wrote with the same power and the same artistic feeling. The occasion of his writing this letter to Mr. Grundy was his wish to obtain some employment in connection with the railway, and he made this overdrawn confession of his habits and indulgences when at Luddenden Foot, and contrasted them with the great mental, moral, and bodily improvement he had acquired since he left. It was his hope that by this contrast he might make a favourable impression, and that Mr. Grundy's position with the Messrs. Stephenson might be a means of helping him to some employment suited to his tastes and abilities. But Mr. Grundy could not aid him in this object, which he pursued with all the feverish eagerness of his urgent and impetuous nature. With great vigour of expression he declares, 'I would rather give my hand than undergo again the grovelling carelessness, the malignant yet cold debauchery, the determination to find how far mind could carry body without both being chucked into hell.'

But Branwell, at the time of which I speak, was full of energy and industry; indeed, he could not be idle. He wrote another letter in reply to one he had received from Mr. Grundy, dated June the 9th, 1842. From this we learn that his friend had either not entertained his applications, or was unable to further his interests in the quarter from which employment could come, for he had given discouraging answers. Branwell felt the disappointment keenly, but says that it was allayed by Mr. Grundy's kind and considerate tone. His friend had asked why he did not turn his attention elsewhere. To this Branwell replies that most of his relations are clergymen, and others of them, by a private life, removed from the busy world. As for the church, he declares he has not one mental qualification, 'save, perhaps, hypocrisy,' which might make him 'cut a figure in its pulpits.' He informs Mr. Grundy that Mr. James Montgomery and another literary gentleman, who had lately seen something of his work, wished him to turn his attention to literature. He declares that he has little conceit of himself, but that he has a great desire for activity. He is somewhat changed, yet, although not possessed of the buoyant spirits of his friend, he might, in dress and appearance, emulate something like ordinary decency.

In Leyland's art commissions at Haworth, Branwell took great interest, and in his correspondence considerable activity and industry appear. He wrote, on June the 29th, 1842, to the sculptor, a letter, in which he alludes to the conduct of some gentlemen of the committee at Haworth, who had acted in an unfair way to his friend on a professional matter. He says:—

'I have not often felt more heartily ashamed than when you left the committee at Haworth; but I did not like to speak on the subject then, and I trusted that you would make that allowance, which you have perhaps often ere now had to do, for gothic ignorance and ill breeding; and one or two of the persons present afterwards felt that they had left by no means an enviable impression on your mind.

'Though it is but a poor compliment,—I long much to see you again at Haworth, and forget for half-a-day the amiable society in which I am placed, where I never hear a word more musical than an ass's bray. When you come over, bring with you Mr. Constable, but leave behind Father Matthew, as his conversation is too cold and freezing for comfort among the moors of Yorkshire.'

At the bottom of the sheet on which this letter is written, Branwell has drawn a pen-and-ink sketch of rare merit. The weird waste, which stretches to the horizon, may represent well the lonely wilds of Haworth, overshadowed by the clouds of approaching night, and interspersed with streaks of fading day, among which the crescent moon appears. In the foreground is a group of monuments, one a tomb sunk on its side; and, of the head-stones, one is inscribed with the word 'Resurgam.' Branwell was no mean draughtsman, and that his hand did not shake with the excesses he is represented to have gone through at this period of his life, the delicacy of this elaborate drawing is sufficient proof.

Mr. Constable, mentioned in the letter, was an acquaintance of the sculptor, a gentleman of considerable ability in art and poetry. The conviviality, which Branwell did not consider altogether a dereliction of moral duty, led him to make his quiet and humorous allusion to Father Matthew.

END OF THE FIRST VOLUME.

FOOTNOTES

[1] 'Life of Charlotte Brontë,' chap. ii.

[2] 'Life of Charlotte Brontë,' chap. iii.

[3] 'Life of Charlotte Brontë,' chap. iii.

[4] Gaskell's 'Life of Charlotte Brontë,' chap. iii, 1st edition.

[5] 'Charlotte Brontë, a Monograph,' pp. 20, 21, 22.

[6] 'Emily Brontë,' by A. Mary F. Robinson, 1883, p. 16.

[7] Mrs. Gaskell's 'Life of Charlotte Brontë,' chap. iii.

[8] James's 'History of Bradford,' p. 358.

[9] Gaskell's 'Charlotte Brontë,' chap. iv.

[10] Gaskell's 'Life of Charlotte Brontë,' chap. iv.

[11] 'Life of Charlotte Brontë,' chap. iv.

[12] 'Life of Charlotte Brontë,' chap. v.

[13] Gaskell's 'Life of Charlotte Brontë,' chap v.

[14] 'Life of Charlotte Brontë,' chap. v.

[15] 'Charlotte Brontë, a monograph,' p. 27.

[16] 'Life of Charlotte Brontë,' chap. vi.

[17] Scribner, ii., 18, 'Reminiscences of Charlotte Brontë.'

[18] Reid's 'Charlotte Brontë, a Monograph,' p. 29.

[19] 'Jane Eyre,' chap. xiii.

[20] 'Life of Charlotte Brontë,' chap. vii.

[21] 'The Mirror,' 1872.

[22] 'Athenæum,' June 16th, 1883, p. 762.

[23] Riley's 'History of the Airedale Lodge,' p. 48.

[24] 'Emily Brontë,' p. 64. It may be noted here, to show in some sort what amount of credibility attaches to these representations, that Miss Robinson has placed Branwell's portrait-painting at Bradford subsequent to his tutorship at Broughton-in-Furness, though really he did not go there until a year later.

[25] 'Life of Charlotte Brontë,' chap, xxvii.

[26] Gaskell's 'Life of Charlotte Brontë,' chap. viii.

[27] 'The Death of Leyland's African Bloodhound,' by William Dearden, author of 'The Star-Seer.' London, 1837. (Longmans.)

[28] 'Agnes Grey,' chap. i.

[29] 'Agnes Grey,' chap. i.

[30] The clock mentioned by Branwell was one that stood in a corner of the 'Snug' at 'The Bull,' inside the door of which the landlord—'Little Nosey'—used to chalk up the 'shots' of his guests.

[31] Charlotte Brontë.—Memoir prefixed to 'Wuthering Heights.'

[32] Gaskell's 'Life of Charlotte Brontë,' chap. ix.

[33] 'Pictures of the Past,' by Francis H. Grundy, C.E. (1879) p. 75.

[34] 'Pictures of the Past,' p. 75.

[35] 'Life of Charlotte Brontë,' chap. x.

[36] 'Life of Charlotte Brontë,' chap. x.

[37] 'Pictures of the Past,' pp. 78-79.

[38] 'Emily Brontë,' p. 97.

[39] 'Emily Brontë,' p. 99.

[40] 'Pictures of the Past,' p. 84.

[41] Gaskell's 'Life of Charlotte Brontë,' chap. viii.

[42] 'Unpublished letters of Charlotte Brontë,' *Hours at Home*, vol. xi.